LONDON BRIDGE
OF
FROM EAST TO WEST

DIEV ET MON DROIT

D0586576

Isis

a30118 045643107b

BRIDGES OF BRITAIN

BRIDGES OF BRITAIN

Eric de Maré

B. T. Batsford Ltd   London and Sydney

First published 1954
New and revised edition published 1975
© Eric de Maré 1975
ISBN 0 7134 2925 9

Filmset by Tradespools Ltd, Frome, Somerset
Printed and bound in Great Britain by
Butler & Tanner Ltd, Frome, Somerset
for the publishers B. T. Batsford Ltd
4 Fitzhardinge St, London W1H 0AH
and 23 Cross Street, Brookvale,
NSW 2100, Australia

Contents

1 *Right*, the most
beautiful stone arch
in Britain: a wood-
engraving of William
Edwards' Pont-y-
Pridd of 1750, with
its pierced haunches.

2 *Next page*, the
central tower of the
Forth Railway Bridge
of 1890.

The endpapers show
an engraving of Old
London Bridge by
John Norden.
Unless otherwise
stated, all photographs
are by the author.

1 Introduction

Long out of print and now a book-collector's item, my *Bridges of Britain* was published by Batsford in 1954. Since then a remarkable period of bridge building has occurred here with the laying of new roads. Also since then public interest in the look of things has grown (no doubt stimulated by television) – not least in the buildings and artifacts of the past that are studied under the new discipline of Industrial Archaeology. Hence this revised volume in which the original text has been shortened, fresh words and pictures have been added, and a traveller's glossary provided of the most interesting bridges of all periods to be seen in England, Scotland and Wales.

Any work which helps people to become more aware of their environment must be of some value, and that makes another apology for this book. It is offered as informative entertainment to the layman so that when he moves around the country he will not pass the many bridges he crosses in blind and blasé boredom but, by realising what they mean in terms of social history, human endeavour, and formal beauty, he will stop to contemplate them for a moment and so find pleasure.

Few bridges are ugly. The reason is that a bridge has one uncompromising function – a limitation that makes for purity of form, a purity that can reach beyond practical prosiness to the poetry of structure, whether as an intimate Elizabethan sonnet rich in texture or a grand modern epic of astounding span. If all good design seeks to express the poetry of structure by working beautifully, can its decoration have a place? Decoration must, of course, always be related to structure and enhance its expression by articulation, but in general the bridge designer has rarely called on the sculptor to embellish his creations in that way; the scale of a bridge is often too large to allow decoration to tell and the whole must be effective at a distance. Form, texture, and sometimes colour provide the effect. Most mediaeval bridges are undecorated in themselves, even if the small chapels with which they were often endowed possessed contemporary ecclesiastical stone carving in windows, doors and pinnacles. Renaissance bridges are the most highly decorated we have, their embellishment well integrated with structure in balustrades. carved keystones and cutwaters. (English Bridge at Shrewsbury, for example, would be impoverished by the loss of the vigorous dolphins above the cutwaters, while cast iron of a later period offers some good examples, as on plates 73–5). The eighteenth century produced many small bridges of character to enhance the noblemen's picturesque parks, and there playful decoration was fully justified. Almost no modern bridges are decorated, even when the architect has been called in for obscure reasons to help the engineer, but sometimes across a motorway paint has been applied to a steel span with gay effect.

At their best, bridges can be seen as symbols of architectural purity in which firm construction, function, and pleasing form are combined. As Palladio wrote three centuries ago, 'Bridges ought to have the self-same qualifications as we judge necessary to all other buildings, that they should be commodious, beautiful, and lasting'.

Bridges are symbols in other ways, and that is perhaps why they move us. They touch us at an unconscious level, representing human control of the environment, the handshake, security, mutual aid, resolution of psychic tensions, a monument to tribal

cohesion, a gathering place 'where thousands meet but none can stay'. They represent direction, purpose, and serene stability. Finally they represent time and its passing because bridges make history, not least in their ecological effects on whole regions. As John Buchan wrote:

'The Bridge, even more I think than the Road, is a symbol of man's conquest of nature . . . From the most primitive times it has been a dominant fact in the life of each community. A bridge ruled the lines of traffic. There might be a dozen roads of travel but they all drew to a point at the river crossings. Cities grew up around them, and castles were built to command them. Battles were fought for their possession, and schemes of strategy were based upon them. With them are linked many of the great feats of arms, from Horatius at Rome to Napoleon at Lodi. History – social, economic, and military – clusters more thickly about bridges than about towns and citadels'.

It is not surprising therefore that myths have developed around the activity of bridge building since early times. The gods are always on the watch in their vengeful way and experience has taught that many have malevolent natures which are never more readily stirred than by the human presumption of building bridges to make life easier. 'Every bridge demands a life' is an ancient superstition that is felt even among the workers who construct, often in some peril, the great steel and concrete spans of today. In the old days the river spirits, seeing themselves likely to be deprived of their regular toll of drowning folk when a new bridge was erected at a ford, fought to prevent the comple-

Decoration of bridges
3 *Left,* carved keystone and balustrade on
John Gwynn's Magdalen Bridge, Oxford, of
1779.
4 *Above,* one of the dolphin cut-waters on
English Bridge, Shrewsbury, 1774, also by
Gwynn.

tion of the bridge and to secure as many lives as possible during its construction. To appease them, human sacrifices were deliberately made during building operations. Thus floods, storms, and accidents might be prevented and the vindictive spleen of the gods allayed. Such blood ceremonies are worldwide. An example is recorded in Sir Mark Sykes's *Dar-Ul-Islam* in a legend he heard at Zakho:

'Many years ago workmen under their master were set to build the bridge; three times the bridge fell and the workmen said, "The bridge needs a life". And the master saw a beautiful girl, accompanied by a bitch and her puppies, and he said, "We will give the first that comes by", but the dog and her little ones held back, so the girl was built alive into the bridge, and only her hand with a gold bracelet upon it was left outside'.

Folklore all over the world connects bridge-building with the sacrificial rite. In old China, for instance, an animal was often built into a pier during construction. The old superstition persists, for when the first edition of this book was published Mr W. P. Warner, engineer, wrote: 'I thought the following, which happened as recently as 1939, might be of interest to you. I was supervising the construction of a lifting-span bridge across a river in Assam; an Indian woman brought a live month-old baby to me and asked me to bury it in the concrete foundations, in order that the bridge would be safe for all time. My Indian workmen were most enthusiastic about it, and my flat refusal was not at all well received'.

In the Christian era the monotheistic Devil displaced the numerous evil ones and all over Europe bridges still bear the name of the Prince, who does not insist on the life of a human being; that of a dog will do. He was indeed at one time happy enough to erect a complete bridge overnight in fair exchange for a life. In the Middle Ages, when bridge building had become a holy activity, bridges were blessed in ceremony and sancti-

Structural development
5 *Left,* Post Bridge, Dartmoor, a clapper bridge perhaps 2000 years old of monolithic slabs of granite each about fifteen feet long.
6 *Above right,* the steel Humber Suspension, under construction in 1975, will have a single span of 4626 feet, the longest in the world.

fied by religious emblems; then every bridge bore its cross, if not its chantry or chapel. Thus the Devil could be kept at bay and the traveller proceed safely on his way.

Our country offers no ancient bridges that can compete in size with the great ones of the Continent. We have no Roman viaducts like that at Segovia or the Pont du Gard near Nîmes which awed even the garrulous Rousseau into silence and filled Charles Kingsley with a simple fear. Of mediaeval structures we have nothing to equal France's Pont des Consuls at Montauban, her towered Pont Valentré at Cahors, or her twelfth-century Pont d'Avignon that gave Bénézet his sainthood. Nor have we competed in later years with such dramatic *tours de force* as Aldequela's eighteenth-century viaduct at Ronda in southern Spain. Yet for over a century, from the erection of Iron Bridge across the Severn in 1779 to that of the Forth Railway Bridge in 1889, Britain led the world in bridge design. Then the initiative passed for a time to America and the Continent, notably in the superb concrete bridges of the Swiss Robert Maillart and the Frenchman Eugène Freyssinet, but now we can match in wiry grandeur the suspensions of New York and San Francisco with our estuarial spans of steel across the Firth of Forth and the Severn. A new bridge at present (1975) under construction across the Humber will, indeed, produce the widest suspension span in the world (6), a bridge 1000 feet wider in size than the new suspension linking Europe with the Middle East across the Bosphorus, which, in fact, was designed by a British firm of engineers. Recently our new motorways have generated a number of splendid concrete spans that compare in nobility with any on the Continent or in Scandinavia.

In general however, our bridges are like the national temperament, that is, shy of overstatement. The landscape rarely calls for drama except across the estuaries. The watery countryside mostly needs a host of small bridges and even our most important river, the Thames, nowhere demands the colossal. Like the landscape our bridges are of great variety, and therein lies their special interest. We possess a remarkable heritage, and many a bridge five centuries old and more still continues its useful function, gallantly bearing the weight and fury of modern traffic. We have the doubtful honour, too, of having inaugurated the Industrial Revolution which made modern technology possible in bridge building as in other activities. With that revolution we produced the first iron bridge in the world (58) and the first few of the great civil engineers. Today the country possesses some 200,000 road bridges, which is about one bridge to every mile of roadway, and, until recently at least, the railway system required some 60,000 bridges, mostly built in the Victorian age, an age that produced a greater number of bridges than had existed in Britain before.

Probably the first structures human beings erected were bridges because, as they wandered, easy access across a river or ravine was more important than housing. Back in the misty forests of prehistory the only bridges that existed were those that nature had built, such as the Rainbow Arch in Utah and the Pont d'Arc in France. Arches like these, as well as overhanging stratifications of stone, gave men their first inspiration to build the corbelled arch – not the true arch of voussoirs but a series of overlapping cantilevers. Two other kinds of natural bridge also provided ideas: the fallen tree across a chasm and the looped vine on which to swing across a stream. So four of the basic types of bridge which span the centuries were in natural existence before artificial bridges were attempted: the Beam, the Suspension, the Cantilever, and the Arch – at least the corbelled arch, for the true arch is a human invention. Up in the North, still barren from the Ice Age, rocks and stones were abundant from the grinding of the glaciers, and there streams could often be crossed from stone to stone where these had tumbled. This gave men another notion: the placing of boulders to form stepping stones where they were needed. (The Latin *pons*, a bridge, may derive from *ponere*, to place). A development would have been the piling of stones into piers across which monoliths could be placed to form a so-called clapper bridge. Such were the first multi-span bridges.

From the simple trunk thrown across a stream eventually developed that sophisticated bridge Robert Stephenson built in the middle of the nineteenth century to carry railway trains through two enormous rectangular iron tubes across the Menai Straits – a pure, if eccentric, beam type (76–78). So also, in effect, is the great trussed railway bridge, known as the Royal Albert (79), that Brunel designed to cross the Tamar at Saltash.

Of cantilever constructions, the Forth Railway Bridge (83) is the most notable example of modern times, with its great double, balanced cantilevers supporting short suspended beam spans between them. The first modern cantilever of iron, however, was erected in 1867 across the River Main at Hassfurt in Germany with a centre span of 425 feet, its designer being Heinrich Gerber. Many fine cantilevers can be seen in the new reinforced concrete spans which often look deceptively like low arches.

The suspension type no doubt first occurred in southerly lands, where having learned to plait and weave, men fashioned ropes made from liana plants and bamboo which they tied to tree trunks on either side of a river in order to swing across hand over hand. There followed a more useful structure of two strands crossed by woven mats to

Stone and iron
7 *Left,* Bakewell Bridge, Derbyshire, a particularly complete and regular mediaeval example of pointed stone arches.
8 *Right,* Britannia Railway Bridge across the Menai Straits of 1850 by Robert Stephenson. Its iron tubes make this a beam bridge.

form a pathway with handrails on each side. (Marco Polo described the making of bamboo bridge cables 300 paces long). The final development was the flat roadway hanging from the curved catenaries, the kind we build now of steel cables but one which was built with different materials far away and long ago by primitive societies in the Himalayas.

A Chinese record of the 7th century A.D. mentions the use of iron chains for suspension bridges built in the Indus valley, but the first suspension in Europe was a bridge of iron chains at Market Harborough; it is mentioned in an Act of 1721 while a map of the town published in 1776 marks the Chain Bridge across the Welland there. A chain suspension bridge only two feet wide, called Winch Bridge, was erected across the Tees near High Force in 1741; this spanned 59 feet. In these early types the floor was laid directly on to the chains. The suspension having a suspended and level roadway was conceived by the American James Finley in 1801, his first patent bridge of this kind being built in 1816. The following year John and Thomas Smith erected a chain suspension across the Tweed at Dryburgh in Roxburghshire and they claimed that it was the first of its sort in Britain; here the chains were made of rods ten feet long with welded eyes and coupling links, forming a span of 261 feet. It cost £500.

The main credit for the development of the iron suspension must go to Captain Brown, RN (1776–1852), later Sir Samuel Brown, who designed the famous Chain Pier at Brighton, completed in 1823 (100). Brown invented an improved way of making links for iron cables which led to the introduction of chain cables in the Navy. He next invented that type of flat iron link used in early suspension bridges which he patented in 1817 and which allowed suspensions to be of much larger span than before. However, without Cort's method of producing wrought iron, first used in 1784, the suspension could not have developed as it did. In 1820 Brown built the first large suspension in the country, wide enough to take carriages: Union Bridge spanning the Tweed near Berwick (123). Six years later the first mail coach from London to Holyhead passed over the new Menai Bridge, Thomas Telford's masterwork with a central span of 579 feet, the largest suspension bridge yet erected (68, 125). The next development was the application of steel cables in place of chains by the Roeblings in the USA.

A rare combination of cantilever and suspension, sometimes called the cable cantilever, is exemplified by Ordish's Albert Bridge, Chelsea, completed in 1873 (55), and in the modern case of the George Street Bridge, Newport (92). This type seems to have been invented by the Frenchman Poyet and the first example was Captain Napier's King's Meadow Bridge of 1817 which crossed the Tweed below Peebles with a span of 110 feet.

The arched bridge works in the opposite way to the suspension – that is not by tension but by compression. (A beam is in compression in its upper part and in tension below). The discovery of the true arch is attributed to the Sumerians who used sun-baked bricks placed side by side in a ring of radiating voussoirs or tapering wedges. So structure was brought alive, seeming to be always at work in that the weight above the crown is perpetually transferred down through each voussoir to the springings and abutments – an invention of immense importance made around the year 4000 B.C. (From the Babylonians has come the visionary legend of the great single span of brickwork jumping 660 feet across the Euphrates to link two palaces). The arch itself with the joints all pointing to a centre does all the work and if a level road is built above it the spaces on each side between road and arch, called spandrels, can be either solid or open.

The semi-circular Roman arch has limitations because the wider it is the higher

Cantilever and Catenary
9 *Left*, contemporary sketch to show how the Forth Railway Bridge works with balanced cantilevers supporting short beams.

10 *Below*, a project for a suspension chain bridge with road supported above the catenary instead of being hung below it, of a type which does not need two towers. (From Weale's *Bridges*, 1843).

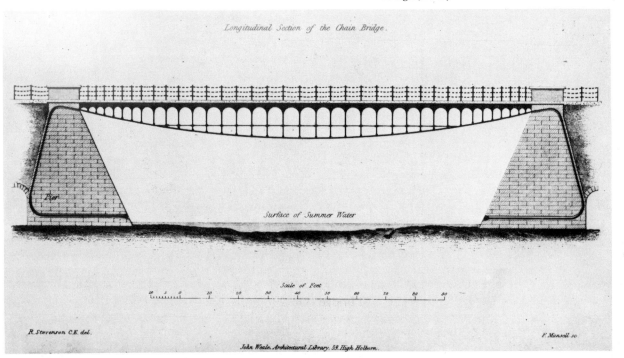

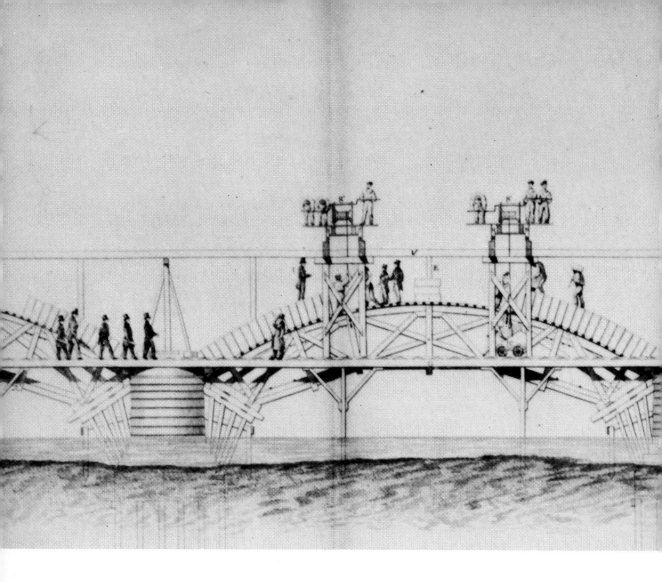

it must be. Small arches in a series of spans can make a long low bridge but with a single semi-circular arch of size the roadway may have to be sloped at each end with ramps; hence the hump-backed bridge of the English countryside. The great French engineer, Perronet (1708–94), who has been called the father of modern bridge building, solved the hump problem by turning the arc into a low, elegant semi-ellipse, a system that greatly increases the pressures of the splaying forces on the abutments at either end of the bridge; in between, of course, each ellipse will press against its neighbour in mutual aid. Perronet, indeed, designed bridges with a rise to span ratio of 1:10. Grosvenor Bridge over the Dee at Chester, opened in 1834, is a product of Perronet's innovations in its possession of the largest pure masonry span in Britain, being 200 feet long with a rise of only 40 feet.

Some steel bridges of today may seem to be arched as in the bowstring girder type, but in fact they are tied so that they really act like huge skeletal beams with the weights going straight down at each end. The new one at Runcorn is an example (89).

Two eccentric types of bridge are the pontoon and the lifting, or movable. The

11 Detail from an engraving showing the building in 1832 of Hutcheson Bridge, Glasgow, of elliptical stone arches, designed by Robert Stevenson (not to be confused with Stephenson) who also designed the chain bridge shown on the previous page. (From Weale's *Bridges*).

pontoon would be a beam bridge using floating boats instead of piers resting on the river bed. Cyrus commanded the laying of the first pontoon bridge on record, while his father's counsellor, Darius, organised the erection of the fabulous bridge of boats, 1000 yards long, by which an army of over half a million men (or so they say) was able to advance, and subsequently retreat, across the Bosphorus. According to legend, Xerxes, son of Darius, built an even more remarkable military bridge, a double row of 360 anchored ships spanned by planks and earth. Today armies still build pontoon bridges and these tend to be of plywood floats spanned by planks.

An important type of movable bridge is the bascule (evolved from the drawbridge of the moated mediaeval castle), in which one span can be lifted to allow the passage of tall ships. Old London Bridge had such a bascule between two of its piers. The canals of the early industrial era possess many bridges which can be lifted by pulling on a chain. At Barton, where the first of the important canals, that of the Duke of Bridgewater, crosses the River Irwell, the huge nineteenth-century iron bridge which replaced Brindley's

aqueduct of stone when the Manchester Ship Canal was dug, can be swung on a pivot still full of water to allow ships to pass (62). At Newcastle is another iron example that pivots. The most important movable bridge in Britain, however, is Tower Bridge where two bascules can be lifted to allow ships to enter the Pool of London; at first the power was hydraulic but lately it has become electric. A special type which has a moving part is the transporter where a carriage to take people and vehicles is suspended from a beam at a high level to allow shipping to pass below at any time, as in the Middlesbrough example (121) or the elegant white elephant at Newport (17).

The oldest existing bridge in the world belongs to the Aegean culture which preceded the Greek. It is a small slab structure of stone of single span across the Meles River in Smyrna, not more than 40 feet long. Homer used it, and St Paul too, nearly nine centuries later. The Greeks built very few bridges and these were mainly similar small slab structures; they hardly needed many bridges for they travelled mostly by sea.

Next to our own, the Roman civilization was the greatest bridge-building epoch in history, and the one from which the European tradition developed – directly, if crudely, in the Middle Ages, and at a remove in the return to classical forms in Renaissance years. The Romans took over the true arch from the Etruscans, using stone, marble, brick and mass concrete; they used timber too and built a bridge of timber across the Thames when they founded *Londinium*. In Britain no doubt the Romans used timber for most of their bridging, for the material was abundant all around; so little remains in our country of Roman bridges except a small rustic arch here and there or a broken causeway glittering beneath the water where once the ordered legions came and went. But many Roman examples still stand on the Continent to impress us with their virility, a notable one being that built for the Emperor Trajan at Alacantra in Spain with a centre arch of 78 feet span.

Like the builders of the Middle Ages the Romans also regarded bridge construction as something of a religious activity. Those who built the ancient *Pons Sublicius*, the first to span the Tiber, are believed to have belonged to a religious body called *Collegium Pontifices*, headed by the *Pontifex Maximus*, Greatest Builder of Bridges. This body developed social power and came to control all those roads and bridges which were essential to the coherence of the empire; so powerful did it become in the end that the Roman Emperors (and later the Popes) assumed the title of *Pontifex Maximus*.

When the Roman Empire fell many of the old skills were lost. Yet some were retained, not least by the Benedictine monasteries which helped more than most to evolve a new culture from the confusion. Among the skills preserved was the making of artificial stones from clay when stone was scarce, so that in Scandinavia today bricks are still called Monk Stones.

As Church organization established some order after the Dark Ages, a building boom began throughout Europe in roads and bridges as well as in cathedrals, churches and monasteries. Religious bridge building fraternities were formed and then the stimulus of the Crusades brought new and glamorous ideas like the pointed arch to create the evolving splendour of Gothic vaulting by replacing the heavy and restrictive round arch and square bay of the Norman or Romanesque style. In spite of the uncertainties of travel a surprising amount of movement had developed by the thirteenth century; roads of a sort were built and many of the old straight Roman roads, if patchy and decrepit, remained in use. This stimulated the erection of a multitude of crude but solid bridges throughout Europe. The War Bridge with its defensive tower and the Chapel Bridge were

Wide arches
12 *Left,* Grosvenor Bridge, Chester, of 1823, designed by Thomas Harrison, has the widest masonry arch in Britain at 200 feet.

13 *Below,* a contemporary engraving of Brunel's viaduct at Maidenhead carrying the Great Western Railway across the Thames with the two widest pure brick arches in Britain.

the significant types along the mediaeval roads, two of the most famous being St Bénézet's at Avignon and Peter of Colechurch's at London, both erected in the twelfth century with chapels rising at their centres.

Compared with the splendid feats of stone engineering in church building, the mediaeval bridges are surprisingly ponderous, relying for stability on brute mass and built so that if one arch failed the neighbouring arches would remain standing on their own. Nevertheless they charm us with their bold, unpretentious austerity, their rich patina and their casual asymmetry. They show two innovations: the building of road recesses which often continue the angular cutwaters up to parapet level where pedestrians could retreat from passing carts and quadrupeds, and the ribbed arch which could save a third of the tooled masonry work and could reduce dead weight and thrusts on piers. The ribbed arch consists of parallel ribs spanned by stone slabs which in their turn support rough masonry up to road level. Twizel Bridge in Northumberland with its graceful single arch is an outstanding example of ribbed construction (24).

The old mediaeval bridge of London requires a special mention now because for centuries it gave life to the City; London was in effect the parasite of the bridge. Without the wooden structure the Romans built at the same place London would, in fact, not have come into being. And in its mediaeval form with its houses, shops, its fair chapel, its gateways, its drawbridge, its great starlings like small pointed islands that protected the piers from buffeting and scouring, its thudding waterwheels, its roaring waters and its ceaseless bustle, it was a wonderful, noisy structure – the key to the City and the pride and emblem of the nation. By its means London was linked not only to the fertile farms of the southern counties but to the whole of the Continent. For over six centuries London had no other crossing and to its citizens it was their greatest vested interest.

This was the first great stone bridge to be erected in these islands. Begun in 1176

Rising bridges

14 *Left*, a drawbridge at Whitchurch across the Welsh section of the Shropshire Union Canal.

15 *Above*, Tower Bridge, London, last bridge before the sea, completed in 1894 with two rising bascules that allow ships to enter the Pool.

on piles of elm wood spanned by oak planks, it replaced the earlier structure of elm. It took 33 years to complete under the direction of Peter, priest and chaplain of St Mary's of Colechurch in the Poultry. It had 20 spans, the seventh being a wooden drawbridge and the rest irregular pointed arches. (Those who want to know its complete history must turn to Gordon Home's enthralling *Old London Bridge*). Owing to its broad piers and starlings it was as much a weir as a bridge, and as a dam that slowed down the ebbing water (with a 5-foot drop as the river ebbed) it created those famous Frost Fairs on frozen water that occurred above-bridge during cold winters through the centuries.

London Bridge was at its finest in Tudor days when Nonesuch House was built on it, a kind of timber-framed block of luxury flats inhabited by noblemen – 'a beautiful and chargeable peece of worke' according to Stow. At that time Norden made engravings of the bridge and described it as 'adorned with sumptuous buildings and statlie and beautiful houses on either side, inhabited by wealthy citizens and furnished with all manner of trades comparable in itself to a little Citie, whose buildings are so artificially contrived,

Transporters
16 *Above,* a rope and timber job from a book of 1590.

17 *Right,* Newport Transporter Bridge built of steel in 1906. This type allows ships to pass below at any time without the need to raise a roadway.

and so finely combined, as it seemeth more than an ordinary streete, for it is as one continuall vaute or roofe, except certain voyde places reserved from buildings, for the retire of passengers from the danger of carres, carts and droves of cattell, usually passing that way'.

In 1757 all the houses were removed and the two central arches were widened into one Great Arch, all according to the designs of George Dance, the City Surveyor. But its end was near and in 1824 Rennie's new London Bridge was begun just to the west of the old structure (19). This was opened in 1831 and three years later no vestige remained of the fabulous old bridge which had served London for so long.

The Renaissance refined the arch and brought advances in building techniques, notably in mechanical plant and in caissons for foundation laying as a development by prefabrication of the old timber cofferdams. The most beautiful of Renaissance bridges was the Santa Trinita in Florence by Michelangelo and Ammanati which was destroyed in the Second World War but has been rebuilt in facsimile. The most famous of Renaissance bridges on the Continent is Da Ponte's Rialto Bridge that spans 88 feet across the Grand Canal at Venice; like Pontevecchio, Florence, High Bridge, Lincoln, and Pulteney Bridge, Bath, (47) it is one of the few housed bridges left in the world.

By the eighteenth century, knowledge had become so systemized that the civil engineer with his specialized skill took the place of the architect in designing bridges; old Westminster Bridge, London's second crossing, was designed by a Swiss engineer called Labelye in the middle of the eighteenth century (20, 48). The best works of that century were

those of Jean Perronet, whose finest work was the Neuilly Bridge near Paris with its long, low, leaping arches (demolished 1938). As already noted, Perronet developed the segmental masonry arch to a high refinement and was able to reduce the thrusts on piers by making each arch push against its neighbour so that the whole structure could become lighter and continuous.

The Renaissance developed the truss largely because timbers long enough to span 60 feet or more were becoming increasingly hard to obtain. The truss uses the principle of triangulation, the triangle being the only figure in geometry whose shape cannot be distorted unless one of its parts is changed in length. The truss became of growing use for temporary centering when masonry arches were built, but the great days of the permanent wooden truss began when the brothers Grubenmann, Swiss village carpenters of the eighteenth century, erected their superb timber structures; they continued in the nineteenth century when the American pioneers spanned the rivers with timbers cut from the primeval forests (often roofing their spans against the snow). The greatest span achieved with timber trusses in the USA was the roofed Colossus over the Schuylkill at Fairmont, Pennsylvania; built in 1812 to the design of an architect, Louis Wernwag, it achieved a single span of 340 feet, only 50 feet less than the timber span the Grubenmanns had built at Wettingen in 1758.

The truss was later developed in iron when the early railers were busy both here and in the States, the first application being Sir John M'Neile's bridge on the Dublin–Drogheda railway with a span of about 40 feet. The most splendid development of the iron truss, however, came with the building of Crumlin Viaduct across the Ebbw Vale in 1857 (lately demolished) which applied the Warren triangular lattice girder (82).

To conclude this sketchy world survey we must point to the development of navigational aids in the seventeenth century as the true start of the Industrial Revolution: to the full application of the steam engine by Watt, particularly in pumping to allow deeper mining than even Newcomen's early pumps could accomplish; to the digging of the English canals which, by linking iron with coal, made the Revolution possible; to the improvement of roads after the Turnpike Acts; to the arrival of the railways; to Bessemer's method of steel production, and finally to the rediscovery of concrete and its unprecedented combination with steel to form reinforced concrete.

Up to the end of the nineteenth century most ferrous structures were of cast or wrought iron and, even though Bessemer had patented his steel-making process in 1856, steel was not generally used for bridges until the end of the century, the Forth Railway Bridge of 1889 (83) being an early example (if one excepts the eccentric case of the suspension span of steel chains crossing the Danube at Vienna designed by Von Mites and built as far back as 1828 before Bessemer's invention had been conceived).

Steel brought a revolution, for it is stronger, less brittle, than iron and it is almost perfectly isotropic, that is to say it will react under stresses uniformly in every direction so that computations in its use can be exact. A great aid to steel production towards the end of the nineteenth century was Martin and Seimens open-hearth process. High tensile steel is the latest development and this has engendered such slim suspensions as the

18 *Left*, engraving of London's old mediaeval bridge as it was in 1745 shortly before the houses were demolished. This remained the City's only crossing for over five centuries.

19 *Below*, the opening of Rennie's new London Bridge in 1831, engraved from a painting by Stanfield. It has been rebuilt in Arizona.

20 *Above*, an aquatint of Labelye's
Westminster Bridge of 1750 with its fifteen
stone arches. This was London's second
crossing.

21 *Right*, by way of structural contrast and a
result of two centuries of technical developments, this elegant footbridge of post-tensioned
concrete across the A2 at Swanscombe, Kent,
has a three-hinged arch with cantilevered side
spans; it was designed by J. A. Bergg
(Photograph: Colin Westwood).

Severn Bridge. Greater strength and rigid, continuous structure in steel has also come
with the welded joint whereby the old, weakening rivets and bolts can be discarded. As
well as metal fatigue, corrosion has raised some difficulties in the use of steel, for steel
rusts far more quickly than iron; the Forth Railway Bridge, for instance, must be con-
tinually painted – work that takes three years to complete and then starts all over again.

The Romans used mass concrete made with natural hydraulic binders, and this
material has been rediscovered fairly recently – initially in the Portland cement used by
Smeaton in his Eddystone lighthouse. In 1824 Joseph Aspdin, a Yorkshire bricklayer,
invented an artificial cement which is the basis of modern concrete, and in 1877 the first
bridge of mass concrete was built with three arches across the River Axe at Seaton in
Devonshire to a design by a civil engineer named Philip Branna. But concrete did not come
into its own until married to steel. The originator of reinforced concrete seems to have
been W. B. Wilkinson, a plasterer, who in 1865 erected a fire-resisting cottage in that
composite fabric. From that small start of just over a century ago reinforced concrete has
become the most important building material in the world today, not least in bridging.

When steel and concrete are combined, the concrete takes the compression, for it
is weak in tension, while steel rods incorporated in the lower part of a beam, for example,
take the tension, thus greatly lightening structure. With improved steels this combination
of materials has been much advanced by stretching the rods or wires within the concrete
with jacks by pre-stressing or post-tensioning. This has lightened structure even further
and to a point of great elegance. The invention must be credited to Eugène Freyssinet of

2 Mediaeval

Almost nothing remains of bridges in Britain built before the Middle Ages except a few clapper, or cromlech, bridges, which, as a type, are prehistoric, and a few Roman relics like the bridge abutments of stone at Chollerford, Northumberland. In the early Middle Ages fords were more common than bridges at river crossings, as the large number of place-names ending with the suffix -ford indicate, and it is just at those points where rivers possessed bridges or dependable fords that towns grew up. Rivers, with their fords and bridges, have formed our whole road system and a glance at a map will show that almost every old town in the land is situated on or near a river – Malvern and Shaftesbury being rare exceptions.

Two points on any river become important in history, for at those points towns have developed: first, the point nearest the mouth where a bridge could be built and an inland port established; secondly, the lowest point on the river which was always possible to ford even in the worst weather. In the case of the Thames, London was the first and Wallingford the second. (When William the Conquerer took London he went all the way to Wallingford to cross the Thames and then eastward along the north of the river).

The mediaeval builders were well supplied with fairly heavy plant such as water-driven hammers for making wrought iron, water-driven pumps, hoisting engines, tackles, and rams on shear-legs. Main foundations consisted of timber piles shod with iron on which boards were laid (hardwood sunk in mud does not rot). Stone, set in lime mortar, was mostly ashlar which came either from local quarries or was carried from a distance by water, even from abroad.

Not only the monasteries, but also town corporations, landowners and religious guilds undertook the building of bridges; the King himself was directly concerned and no bridge of stone could be erected without his consent. Finance came, in the main, from private bequests, including episcopal indulgences, and maintenance was often covered by tolls. Bridges were frequently 'farre in decay for lakke of tymely reparacion', and frequent catastrophes may be a reason why mediaeval bridges, built at a period that produced such beautiful, aetherial and intricate workmanship in stone elsewhere, were so often rough, heavy, and ready structures; to lavish fine craftsmanship upon them would have been discouraging, so that bridges were perforce utility structures only – if we except the attendant chapels and chantries.

Every mediaeval bridge had its cross, but of bridge crosses now only a stump remains here and there to mark the passing of the Roundheads. Some bridges were further dedicated by a chapel attended by one or more Bridge Priests. Only three with chapels remain: at Wakefield (27) and Rotherham (28), both in Yorkshire, and at St Ives in Huntingdonshire (26). Of these Wakefield is the least debased and, as its Decorated work shows, it belongs to the fourteenth century.

Of war bridges two good examples survive: Warkworth in Northumberland and Monnow Bridge at Monmouth (29), both of which retain their defensive towers. Stirling Bridge, Scotland – at one time the key to the Highlands and of great strategic importance – remains a fine structure but has lost its gateway (30).

Scotland retains a fair number of mediaeval bridges, perhaps because the demands of modern traffic have been less pressing there than elsewhere in Britain. Wales has its well known bridge across the Dee at Llangollen, part of which has survived from 1131. Two bridges of the southwest deserve special mention on account of their lengths: Wade-bridge in Cornwall with 15 arches and Bideford in Devon with 24. The strangest and most haunted of all Gothic bridges is that at Crowland in Lincolnshire (31). Called Trinity Bridge, or Three-Ways-to-Nowhere, it may have been erected by the local abbey as a symbol of the Trinity rising above the flat and watery landscape.

The thoroughfares the bridges served included many a straight old Roman road, and all roads were busy enough with men, horses, and the heavy, lumbering, two-wheeled carts of the peasants. Now and then a horse litter would pass, or a lordly four-wheeled carriage, awkward but luxurious, gilded, carved, brightly painted, and protected by a hooped awning of fine tapestries. A prelate would ride by, a peripatetic London magistrate on his way to the county court, a bishop with his train, a merchant or farmer on his way to market, a wandering minstrel, a journeyman mason or carpenter, a herbalist quack, a group of jugglers, a running messenger or a knight at arms with his retinue. A tied serf in his leather jerkin would stop his tilling for a moment on some rustic strip to stare in wonder as the King rode by followed by a splendid throng and a host of lesser parasites – not so rare a sight as might be imagined, for the Court travelled incessantly on state affairs from town to town, from manor to manor, accompanied by cartloads of rolled documents. With all this movement bridge building was important in mediaeval times.

22 *Page 28*, Defence tower of the old mediaeval Welsh Bridge at Shrewsbury from a romantic etching of 1820. The bridge no longer exists.

23 *Below*, mediaeval transport in the form of a carriage of the fourteenth century depicted in the Luttrell Psalter.
24 *Right*, the 90-feet arch of Twizel Bridge, Northumberland, longest mediaeval span in England, with its economical ribbed construction.

Ribbed arches
25 *Above*, Ludford Bridge, Ludlow.
26 *Right*, the chapel bridge of St Ives,
Huntingdonshire.

Chapel bridges
27 *Left*, Wakefield Bridge, Yorkshire, with its Decorated fourteenth-century chapel.
28 *Below*, the chapel of 1483 at Rotherham Bridge, Yorkshire, with its pinnacles and castellations.

War bridges
29 *Above*, Monnow Bridge, Monmouth, built
in 1272 with a tower but widened at a later
date.
30 *Right*, Stirling Bridge of about 1400 was the
key to the Highlands and once possessed a
tower.

3 Post-Reformation

As the unifying power of the Mother Church declined and nationalism in its modern form was born, the defensive tower and the chapel ceased to concern the bridge builder, partly because his work was now secular and partly because the war bridge had become obsolete with the discovery of gunpowder. Renaissance trends eventually brought immense developments but they were delayed for two centuries. In Britain the years between the mid-sixteenth and mid-eighteenth centuries were not great bridging years, although with the growth of trade many small structures for pack-horse trains were erected, the longest surviving one being Essex Bridge, crossing the Trent with fourteen arches at Great Haywood in Staffordshire.

The eighteenth century was more active, mainly in the latter part when the canals were begun and after the General Turnpike Act of 1773 came – with the help of men like Metcalf and Macadam, and later Smeaton and Telford – to improve roads that had everywhere decayed into an appalling condition of potholes and mud, and to bring before long the brief, picturesque epoch of the stage coach before the railways arrived.

The foundation and upkeep of bridges by religious bodies were necessarily abandoned at the Dissolution, and in 1530 an Act was passed that placed the same responsibility on counties for the maintenance of bridges as was borne by parishes for the upkeep of highways, though small bridges were often maintained by parishes. When bridges were rendered unsafe by storm or flood, private individuals could repair the damage on their own initiative and later claim their expenses in court.

It is impossible to draw a firm line in time between the eighteenth-century works of the architect and the nineteenth-century works of the engineer – between this chapter and the next. The adapted Roman mode of Palladio and his followers with its classical grammar was often the work of the new professional man the Renaissance had produced, the educated architect. His was scholarly work, precise, dignified, carefully proportioned, and far less weighty than the Gothic works of the master masons, but in technique it showed at first few revolutionary advances on mediaeval structure. After the architect came the early engineer, often a craftsman, to develop bridge construction with new methods and materials. Telford was a mason and Smeaton trained himself as a craftsman.

Two bridges of strong baroque character still stand: Vanbrugh's uncompleted Grand Bridge across the lake on the axis approach to Blenheim Palace in Oxfordshire, so bold and extravagant that the Duchess of Marlborough declared in high dudgeon that it 'passed all men's understanding' (41) and General Wade's fine military bridge with its four obelisks at Aberfeldy, one of many built at the same time to open up the Highlands (37).

To the eighteenth century belongs the beautiful arch by William Edwards at Pont-y-Pridd with its span of 140 feet and its haunches pierced with tunnels to lighten the structure and allow the passage of flood water. This principle has reached its latest development in the open spandrels of modern concrete bridges (95). The great arch of 149 feet span built at Ceret in the fourteenth century has the earliest surviving open spandrels.

Important eighteenth-century bridges are those designed by the architect John Gwynn: Magdalen at Oxford (3, 33), English at Shrewsbury (4), Worcester, and Atcham (50). Others include Robert Adam's housed Pulteney Bridge at Bath (47), Labelye's Westminster (demolished 1851 and the first case in Britain where caissons were used for the foundations) (20, 48), Mylne's noble Blackfriars with its nine elliptical arches (third across London's river, demolished in the 1860s) (49), Smeaton's bridges at Perth, Coldstream (38), and Banff, and, on the upper Thames, Taylor's Maidenhead, Paine's Richmond and Chertsey, Hayward's Henley, and two elegant toll bridges above Oxford at Swinford and Lechlade whose designers are unknown. All these were built of stone in classical style.

Some notable Georgian bridges stand in the parks of the aristocracy: the elaborate, roofed Palladian one at Wilton designed by the Architect Earl, ninth Lord Pembroke (44), Robert Adam's swaggy, balustered one of three arches with its weir at Kedleston Hall, Derbyshire (45), James Paine's classical one with niches and statues at Chatsworth, Derbyshire, John Soane's simple, single span at Tyringham, Buckinghamshire (42), and the curious little Hindoo folly, with a divine and frondy grot beneath it, by Cockerell and Repton, at Sezincote, Gloucestershire (43).

The Cambridge Backs display a delightful range of small post-Reformation bridges, the two oldest being of the seventeenth century and the most sophisticated and highly decorated examples of the period in the country: Clare (52) and St John's. The latter, built about 1698, has been attributed to Wren but is more likely to have been designed by his assistant Hawksmoor. Trinity, designed by James Essex, was built in 1766 in an elegant way with parapets ending in horizontal curls (53–4). All have three segmental arches. A pleasing eighteenth-century bridge is Queen's (51), one of several Mathematical Bridges of timber which Essex erected in and around Cambridge.

The two finest bridges of the eighteenth century, already mentioned, are the second and third that London acquired: Labelye's Westminster with its 15 diminishing semicircular arches of Portland stone and the darker Purbeck (20, 48), and Robert Mylne's Blackfriars (49) which applied the economical elliptical French arch in its nine spans of which the centre one was 100 feet wide. Later, Mylne was among those who submitted ideas for a new London Bridge, but finally John Rennie's design was accepted and carried out (19); and with Rennie we come to the Great Age and the next chapter.

33 *Page 40*, Magdalen Bridge, Oxford, designed by Gwynn and completed in 1779. The tower of Magdalen College is in the background.

34 *Left*, a wood engraving of a packhorse convoy, an important means of transport before the Industrial Revolution.

35 *Above*, Stopham Bridge, crossing the Arun in Sussex, was built in Tudor times; its central arch was built high, possibly at a later date, to permit the passage of boats.

36 A stone packhorse bridge of 1822 crossing the Nidd near Burnt Yates in the West Riding.

37 One of the few baroque bridges in Britain
is that at Aberfeldy which crosses the Tay in
Perthshire; it is one of General Wade's 40
eighteenth-century military bridges built to
open up the Highlands.

Pierced bridges. Tunnels through the spandrels or haunches both lighten weight on foundations and allow passage of flood-water.

38 *Below*, Smeaton's Coldstream Bridge of 1766 crossing the Tweed on the Scottish border.

39 *Right*, Pant-y-Goytre Bridge over the Usk, Monmouthshire, built about 1821 by John Upton of Gloucester.

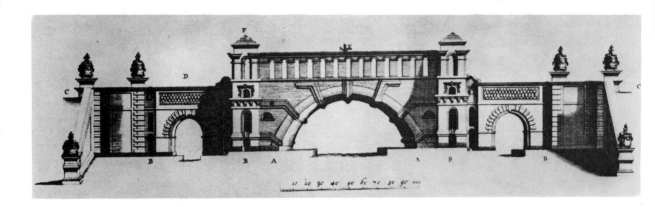

48

Park bridges
40 *Left*, the Grand Bridge at Blenheim built
for the first Duke of Marlborough in 1711, a
piece of uncompleted baroque theatricality by
Sir John Vanbrugh designed to contain rooms
below the road and an arcade above it.
41 *Top left*, a contemporary engraving of the
design as intended.
42 *Top right*, John Soane's single-arch at
Tyringham Park, Buckinghamshire.
43 *Right*, the little bridge, with fern filled grot
below, inspired by the Elephant Caves of India,
at Sezincote House, Gloucestershire, designed
by Samuel Cockerell about 1805.

44 The elaborate roofed Palladian bridge at
Wilton Park, Wiltshire, built in 1737 by the
ninth Lord Pembroke. Copies with variations
stand both at Stow and Prior Park, Bath.
(Photograph: Reece Winstone)

Adam bridges
45 *Left*, Robert Adam's bridge with weir at Kedleston Park, Derbyshire.
46 *Below*, Aray Bridge, Inverary, with pierced spandrel.
47 *Right*, the housed Pulteney Bridge, Bath, of 1769. (Photograph: Leighton Gibbins)

54

Georgian road bridges

48 *Top left,* an arch of Labelye's Westminster Bridge completed in 1750, from a painting by Samuel Scott, the English Canaletto. The bridge stood for only a century.

49 *Below left*, an engraving of Robert Mylne's Blackfriars Bridge under construction in 1766.

50 *Below*, Atcham Bridge, Shropshire, John Gwynn's most beautiful structure completed in 1776 as one of the three he built across the Severn.

At the Cambridge Backs
51 The timber Mathematical Bridge at Queen's College erected in 1749 to the design of James Essex. Reconstructed in 1902; sometimes called Newton's Bridge; also attributed to one called Etheridge.

52 Clare Bridge of about 1640, the oldest and
perhaps the most beautiful along the Backs,
designed by Thomas Grumbold. (Photograph:
J. Allan Cash)

At the Cambridge Backs
Trinity Bridge of 1760 by James Essex.
53 *Above*, the abutment detail.
54 *Right*, general view of the three elliptical
arches. (Photograph: J. Allan Cash)

4 Industrial Revolution

The marriage of coal and iron conceived the Great Age of British bridge building. It extended from the erection of Ironmaster Abraham Darby's Iron Bridge of 1779 in Coalbrookdale (58–9), the cradle of the Industrial Revolution, to that of the Forth Railway Bridge in 1889 (83–4). The way to heaven now lay not through feudal hangover, land ownership, cultivated leisure for the few, and picturesque landscape, but through hard work, industrial stock, church or chapel attendance, and the dark, Satanic mills of the Manchester Men. The Industrial Revolution began in a practical sense with the opening in 1761 of 'Heav'n-taught' Brindley's canal to link the Duke of Bridgewater's mountain of coal at Worseley with Manchester and Liverpool, thus inaugurating the brief Canal Era. That era produced a few major aqueducts (60, 61) and a host of minor bridges (63–6), almost all of which own a simple beauty arising from their subtle, undecorated curves and arches, their ageing patina of brick and stone, and their unselfconscious functionalism.

With the building of the first public line between Stockton and Darlington, opened in 1825, railways began to oust canals as the main form of heavy transport. (An interesting little bridge on the line, completed in 1824, which combines cast and wrought iron can be seen at the York Railway Museum). Iron brought the steam pump, the steam pump and the canals brought more coal, more coal brought more iron, more iron brought more railways and, with them, the greatest bridging activity this country had yet known. Coal, iron, and steam also stimulated heroic developments in bridge construction; they engendered new aids to building such as heavy mechanical pile drivers, pneumatic caissons for foundations, and steam traction for hauling and raising heavy parts. Technical advances became imperative in railway development, for railways required wide spans of great tensile strength that could bear heavy live loads. Curiously the railways solved their own problem of acquiring adequate supplies of iron ore in that the excavations of tunnels and cuttings revealed unsuspected new ironstone beds, eventually disclosing the great bed which runs in a crescent from the Tees to Weymouth.

The four great engineering names of the age are John Rennie, Thomas Telford, George Stephenson, his son Robert, and Isambard Kingdom Brunel. Rennie (1761–1821) and Telford (1757–1834) were contemporaries whose lives spanned the Canal Era; both were Scotsmen of humble origin who applied their remarkable gifts in an age that offered opportunity to men of vigour and intelligence. Both built road bridges and both built in stone and in iron, but Telford was also responsible for many canals and their crossings and was the more prolific of the two, not least in the use of iron, while Rennie carried the masonry arch to its final development, his most famous bridges being the three he built across the Thames in London: Waterloo in granite (the noblest bridge in the world, according to Canova), Southwark of cast iron and granite, and the new London, also of granite (19). His first important bridge, however, was the one across the Tweed at Kelso, completed in 1803.

Telford's masonry bridges never reached the standard of design or interest of his graceful iron ones. His Buildwas Bridge of 1796 was the third bridge of iron in Britain, the earlier two being Iron Bridge (58) and then Tom (Rights-of-Man) Paine's Wearmouth

Bridge at Sunderland, long since defunct. Among Telford's important masonry feats are Dean Bridge, Edinburgh (124), Mouse Water Bridge, Lanark, and Chirk Aqueduct. His two masterworks, however, contain much iron: the stupendous Pont Cysylltau Aqueduct on the Welsh section of the Shropshire Union Canal (61), and the suspension road bridge across the Menai Straits with its central span of 579 feet (67–8). He built many smaller structures, and, as County Surveyor of Shropshire for most of his working life, he erected no less than 42 bridges in the county, five in iron.

The success of Menai led to other suspensions, notably those at Marlow and Hammersmith (replaced in 1887 by Bazalgette's surviving suspension) by William Tierney Clark (1783–1852), who with his brother Adam built the famous chain bridge over the Danube between Buda and Pest, and that of Brunel (1806–1859) across the gorge at Clifton near Bristol (69). Brunel was also responsible for many bridges on his Great Western Railway, notably the extraordinary affair of fish-bellied girders with their great oval tubes crossing the Tamar at Saltash in Cornwall (79), and the three bridges of red engineering brickwork carrying his line three times across the Thames at Maidenhead (13), Moulsford and Basildon. Brunel also built the iron viaduct (opened in 1851 and demolished in 1958) that took the South Wales Railway across the Wye at Chepstow with a main span largely composed of a tube 309 feet long; no beauty but structurally interesting.

George Stephenson (1781–1848), son of a colliery fireman, who became the pioneering railway engineer, built a number of splendid viaducts, including the Sankey of brick faced with stone, on his Liverpool and Manchester line – a line on which he also erected several smaller structures with cast-iron girders. His son Robert (1819–1859) produced the Royal Border Viaduct of masonry at Berwick, called the Last Act of the Union, the High Level Bridge, Newcastle (87–8), carrying road and rail on two levels by means of six skeleton lintols of iron, cast and wrought, each 125 feet wide, and his tubular iron railway bridges, the Britannia and the Conway (76–8), on the Chester–Holyhead line – the first examples of the flat beam in modern bridge construction. Opened in 1850, the Britannia contained the longest railway span in the world until Roebling completed his Niagara Suspension five years later.

Two great railway bridges must finally be noted: Liddell, Gordon and Kennard's Crumlin Viaduct of iron, partly wrought, across the Ebbw Vale, using the Warren Triangular Girder, which was opened in 1857 and sadly demolished a few years ago (82), and then Baker and Fowler's dinosaur, the Forth Railway, opened in 1890 (83–4). Such great viaducts, awesome in their pride, are the best landscape legacies of the Railway Age.

55 *Page 60*, A tower of the iron Albert Bridge, Chelsea, of 1873 by R. M. Ordish; half suspension, half cantilever, known as the stayed type.

56 *Left*, Stephenson's Rocket, from a Victorian wood engraving, symbolizes transport in the age of steam and iron. The Industrial Revolution brought many structural developments, not least in the laying of foundations such as, *right*, 57, this pneumatic iron caisson of the 1860s. A. iron ballast; B. water ballast; C. lifting chains; D. air lock; E. winch ropes inside columns.

58, 59 Iron Bridge across the Severn in Coalbrookdale, built in 1779 as the first bridge of iron in the world. It was shipped down river in sections from Abraham Darby's iron works and was erected in three months. Total span is 100 feet 6 inches.

60 Cotton-king Oldknow's Marple Aqueduct, Cheshire, carrying the Peak Forest Canal, depicted in an aquatint of 1803.

61 Pont Cysylltau Aqueduct carrying the Welsh
Section of the Shropshire Union Canal across
the Dee. Designed by Thomas Telford and
completed in 1805 with an iron trough
supported on tall stone columns.

62 The Barton Swing Aqueduct carries the
Bridgewater Canal across the Manchester Ship
Canal; it is swung open still filled with 1500
tons of water.

Canal bridges of iron, brick, stone and timber.
63 *Left*, a precast type at Braunston on the Grand Union.
64 *Below left*, at Great Haywood where the Staffordshire and Worcestershire Canal joins the Trent and Mersey.
65 *Right*, a wooden swing bridge on the Gloucester and Berkeley Ship Canal.
66 *Below*, a simple stone bridge on the Macclesfield Canal.

Telford's Suspension Bridge across the Menai Straits between North Wales and Anglesey, opened in 1826, has a span of 579 feet. It was partly reconstructed in 1940 to take modern traffic. See also page 133.

67 *Below*, a close-up of the chains.
68 *Right*, the arched approach on the Anglesey side.

Suspension spans
69 *Top*, Brunel's Clifton Bridge crosses the
Avon Gorge with a span of 702 feet; begun in
1836, it was not completed until 1864.

70 *Above*, Telford's iron Conway Bridge
completed in 1826 with inept towers intended to
harmonize with the architecture of Conway
Castle. On the left of the bridge is Stephenson's
tubular railway bridge.

71 A charming small footbridge of steel built across the Dee at Cambus-o'-May, Aberdeenshire, in 1905; the approach to a suspension bridge, however small, provides a monumental effect by virtue of the framing of one tower by the other.

72 Thomas Page's Chelsea Suspension Bridge
in a print of 1852, showing Wren's Chelsea
Hospital beyond. The bridge was opened in
1858 but was replaced by the present suspension in 1934.

Iron decoration
73 *Top Left*, wrought iron centre of Chepstow Bridge across the Wye, opened in 1816.
74 *Below*, spandrel detail of the cast-iron arch of Telford's Waterloo Bridge at Bettws-y-Coed, built in 1815, the year of the Battle of Waterloo.
75 *Right*, Surrey end of Blackfriars Railway Bridge of 1864.

79

Robert Stephenson's two tubular bridges of
iron.
76 *Left*, the end of Britannia Bridge of 1850
across the Menai Straits with its flanking lions.
77 *Below left*, the Conway Bridge of 1849
(from a contemporary print).

78 A tube of the Britannia under construction
(from a contemporary print).

79 Brunel's strange
fish-bellied girder
railway bridge of 1859
across the Tamar,
known as Saltash, or
Royal Albert, Bridge.

80 The noble
Victorian brick
viaduct at Balcombe
carrying the London–
Brighton line across
the Ouse Valley.

Viaducts
81 *Above,* a pair in hard stone at Chapel-en-le-Frith, Derbyshire.
82 *Right,* Crumlin in the Ebbw Vale, opened in 1857 and demolished in the 1960s. It was important in its early use of the Warren triangular girder.

83, 84 Baker and Fowler's Forth Railway
Bridge of 1890. An early steel bridge, it was
hand-tailored on the spot and consists of three
balanced cantilevers joined by short beams.
The tubes are 12 feet in diameter, and the total
length, with approaches, is over one and a half
miles.

5 Modern

As iron represented the Railway Age so steel and concrete represent the age of the petrol engine. The arch of Iron Bridge (1779) has a span of 100 feet 6 inches. The great steel bow, hinged and trussed, of Bayonne Bridge over the Kill van Kull, New York (1931) has a span of 1652 feet, so beating Sydney Harbour Bridge (opened a few months later) by exactly two feet. Our own Tyne Bridge, Newcastle (1930) with its trussed and tied arch, or bowstring girder, is only 531 feet, but even that is impressive (87, 115). More so is the Runcorn–Widnes Bridge (1961) by Mott, Hay and Anderson, with its span of 1082 feet, which has replaced the old Widnes Transporter across the Mersey (89). An elegant and smaller bowstring with a simple, slender tied arch by the same engineers is the new Scotswood crossing the Tyne with a span of 140 feet, which in 1968 replaced the old suspension of 1831. Such bowstring types are strong and particularly suitable for heavy modern road traffic.

An interesting development is the stayed girder type which is a kind of hybrid of cantilever and suspension. Here the deck is not suspended from a parabola with hangers but from cables sloping down from towers to deck. Since the deck here takes large compression forces, such bridges are unsuitable for spans over 1500 feet. A precedent, as we have seen, is the beloved Albert Bridge, Chelsea, completed in 1873 by the engineer Ordish (55). Two modern examples are the Wye Viaduct and George Street Bridge, Newport, both by Mott, Hay and Anderson (91–2). The Wye Viaduct, which is virtually a continuation of the Severn Suspension, has a stiffened box girder stayed by steel cables stretching down from two slender pillars supported by steel trestles. A larger version of the type is that at Newport with a main span across the Usk of 500 feet, achieved by four tall towers of hollow reinforced concrete and a number of steel wires passing over rollers within the tops of the towers and supporting a deck of boxes made of cellular steelwork.

The two new British bridges which have surprised the world are the great ethereal suspensions of the Forth (93) and the Severn (85, 90, 108), by the engineers Mott, Hay and Anderson in association with Freeman, Fox and Partners. The Forth, which replaced the ferry in 1964, consists of two towers of high tensile steel rising 512 feet and supporting catenary cables of 11,618 galvanized high tensile steel wires wrapped with binder wire and painted. Two Warren truss girders run the full length of the bridge under the deck along the central span of 3300 feet. 30,000 tons of steel were used here as against the 50,000 required for its narrower neighbour, the Forth Railway Bridge. 250 men were employed in its construction as against 4500 for the railway structure, although it must be remembered that in the latter case all steelwork was tailor-made on the site, and that the engineers were taking no chances after the Tay Bridge disaster and so somewhat overbuilt their work.

The Severn Bridge, carrying the London–South Wales motorway that reduces the journey between South-West England and South Wales by 50 miles, was completed in 1966 with a main span 60 feet shorter than that of the Forth. The deck support consists of a shallow box of welded steelwork instead of girders, while the suspenders of wire cable are not vertical but run in a series of triangles. A third large new suspension, but one of far less visual attraction than either the Forth or the Severn, is that crossing the Tamar close to Brunel's Royal Albert Viaduct at Saltash, opened in 1961.

New bridges of reinforced concrete, large and small, have been built in the last two decades in great numbers all over the country. A small example but one of importance is the delightful Garret Hostel footbridge of 1960 at Cambridge designed by the late Anthony Morgan. Spanning 80 feet, it is the first bridge of post-tensioned concrete to have been erected in Britain (109).

Two important concrete bridges now cross London's river: Waterloo (98) and the new New London (99). Waterloo, completed in 1945 by Rendell, Palmer and Tritton, is a beam bridge of five spans looking like an arch type; it is the most graceful London's river possesses. New London, completed in 1973 by Harold King, City Engineer, with Mott, Hay and Anderson, to replace Rennie's granite structure (now re-erected in Arizona) is not visually thrilling but interesting and practical, being composed of four prestressed concrete box beams in precast segments strung together with cables like a string of beads and forming three flat 'arches' that are in fact cantilevers with a central suspended beam, the central span totalling 340 feet.

Of large new concrete bridges of character on the motorways must be mentioned the long one taking the M2 across the Medway at Rochester (96), the arched spans with open spandrels of the Taf Fechan (95) and the Nant Hir on the Heads of the Valleys Road, South Wales, Bridstow Bridge on the Ross Motorway, and the strutted Wentbridge Viaduct on the A1 near Doncaster (97), to say little of the several elevated roads such as the Hammersmith Flyover and the Chiswick–Langley section of the M4. There is also a fine arched, open spandrel example over the Lune to carry the Lancaster bypass. A particularly beautiful concrete bridge is the Clifton crossing the Trent at Nottingham, which like New London Bridge has two cantilevers and a suspended span.

The upper Thames has two important crossings: Runnymede, carrying the Staines bypass with steel arches encased in Portland stone, and Thames Bridge below Maidenhead carrying the M4 on a welded steel span faced with bricks.

As materials grow stronger, structures grow lighter and spans wider. Yet even today, for all their precise calculations and skills, engineers are not infallible; they make mistakes and disasters sometimes occur. A bridge may still demand one life or more, as in the spectacular failure by oscillation of the Tacoma Narrows Bridge in 1940 when a little dog perished.

85 *Page 90*, the Severn Suspension Bridge has a central span of 3240 feet. It was completed in 1966 and shortens the journey between England and Wales by 50 miles.
86 *Left*, a Rolls-Royce Silver Ghost symbolizes the petrol age.

87 *Right*, the Tyne Bridge, Newcastle, a tied arch bridge of 531 feet span opened in 1930. Beyond is a swing bridge of 1876, and beyond that again Stephenson's double-decker High Level Bridge of 1849 which takes road and rail.
88 *Above*, a hinge of the Tyne Bridge.

89 Mott, Hay and
Anderson's Runcorn–
Widnes tied arch, or
bowstring, bridge of
1961 with a span of
1082 feet. This type is
strong in order to
cope with heavy road
traffic. (Photograph:
John Cleare)

New road bridges
90 *Left*, the Severn Suspension under
construction showing the raising of a
prefabricated section of the steel box deck into
place. (Photograph: British Steel Corporation)

Above, two examples of the stayed girder, or
cable cantilever, type.
91 *Top*, the Wye Viaduct which virtually
continues the Severn Bridge on the
Monmouthshire side.
92 *Bottom*, George Street Bridge, Newport.
(Photographs: William Tribe)

93 The Forth Road
Bridge of 1964 has a
span of 3300 feet. The
cables of high tensile
steel wires support
two truss girders.

Reinforced concrete
94 Arup's eccentric Kingsgate footbridge of
1965 across the Wear at Durham University;
the band was built on the bank and swivelled
into position on to its tapering-finger supports.
(Photograph: de Burgh Galwey)

95 Rendel, Palmer and Tritton's Taf Fechan
Bridge, Heads of the Valleys Road, Wales, of
1960 with arch span of 227 feet. (Photograph:
W. E. Middleston)

Reinforced Concrete
96 *Above,* Freeman, Fox's elegant Medway
Bridge of 1963 carrying the M2 near Maidstone, Kent; its prestressed cantilevered
central span is 500 feet, longest of its kind in
the world. (Photograph: Leonard Hill)
97 *Below left,* Maynard Lovell's Wentbridge
Viaduct carrying the A1 near Doncaster; it
required 90 miles of steel tube scaffolding to
erect. (Photograph: Maurice Broomfield)
98 *Below,* Waterloo Bridge, London, completed 1942, is not an arched bridge but a beam
bridge, widest span being 250 feet; facing is of
Portland stone.

99 Harold King's New London Bridge of 1972 which replaced Rennie's stone bridge of 1831. The three spans are of prestressed concrete box beams forming cantilevers with central suspended beams. The main span is 340 feet wide.

105

100 Captain Brown's Chain Pier of 1823 at
Brighton after its destruction by the hurricane
of 1833 (depicted in an engraving of 1842). It
was rebuilt but was finally destroyed in the
storm of 1896.

6 Failures and Fantasies

The pressure of flood water was the main cause of failure in mediaeval times but as piers grew slimmer and spans wider this hazard was lessened. Suspension types have suffered most, mainly on account of oscillation and undulation caused by wind. The disaster of Tacoma Narrows Bridge (Galloping Gertie), which occurred in 1940 only four months after the bridge had been opened, was the most dramatic, and an object lesson to modern engineers throughout the world. Even Telford had some trouble at Menai, and an English disaster occurred on Captain Brown's Chain Pier of 1823 at Brighton, which collapsed in a hurricane in 1833 (facing page) and finally in the great gale of 1896. The only cure for oscillation is to stiffen the deck.

The 1870s and '80s saw a series of failures of iron railway bridges; on the American railroads iron-truss bridges were failing at the rate of 25 a year. Rescue came from two sources: the rapid evolution of metallurgy and of structural engineering as exact sciences, and the use of steel. Britain's worst disaster in iron occurred at the Tay Bridge near Dundee which collapsed less than two years after completion. At over two miles this was the longest railway bridge in the world. Everyone was proud of it, even William McGonagall, Dundee's braggart son and the world's worst poet, who wrote an ode to the bridge. The first stanza, he later admitted, 'will possibly be as much as you can stand':

> *The Tay Bridge is a beautiful span,*
> *And the river Tay runs through it;*
> *A wonderful work by the hands of man,*
> *Many strangers come for to view it.*

Its designer, Thomas Bouch, received the accolade, and then on a Sunday evening, three days after Christmas 1879, a strong gale blew against its 84 spans as a mail train was steaming across it. Thirteen spans collapsed and the train plunged, carriage after carriage, into the icy water with its 80 passengers, none of whom survived. A Board of Trade enquiry found that 'the bridge had been badly designed, badly constructed, and badly maintained'. Four months later, his spirit broken, Sir Thomas Bouch expired.

The subject of bridges that failed in the sense that they were never built would fill another volume, but a few curious, sometimes beautiful, and often grandiose projects must be mentioned in concluding this survey. In 1793 a certain William Bridges designed a splendid affair of masonry, almost a folly, to cross the Avon Gorge at Clifton (104). It had a tall central arch 220 feet high and 180 feet wide to allow tall ships to sail below. Each of the five storeys in its abutments was 40 feet high and contained granaries, a corn exchange, wharfs, storage for coal, a market, a museum and library, a marine school, besides various offices, stables, warehouses and 20 dwellings. Above the arch was a chapel, a tollhouse, a belfry, and, at the very apex, a lighthouse, while in the spandrels two windmills revolved.

A number of schemes for the Clifton Bridge across the Avon Gorge were prepared for a competition, including a Gothic affair by Telford in his old age: in the end even the winning design by Brunel was not executed in its first form (69). Telford also designed a suspension in 1814 to cross the Mersey at Runcorn with a single leap of 1000 feet which appears in an engraving at the end of the *Atlas* of his works; from the look of its gentle catenary it hardly seems viable.

Telford's finest project was his design of 1800 for a new London Bridge, having a single span of 600 feet of iron filigree forming a low arch (105). It was universally admired but apparently problems of approach rendered it impractical and Rennie's duller design was chosen. George Dance the Younger, architect of Newgate Gaol, was associated with Telford in his work as Clerk of City Works, and he produced a proud and imposing lay-out for the development of the Port of London as a whole, which contained a pair of arched bridges with bascules at their centres through which ships could pass (106). Between the two bridges on either bank lay two open places, the Monument dominating the north side and a new obelisk to commemorate the recent naval victories, the south. This monumental scheme has been preserved for posterity in an aquatint of 1800 by William Daniell.

Many small bridges were built to decorate the parks of the landed gentry but others never reached further than the engraver's plate or the architect's drawing. Robert Adam produced one in 1768 for Bowood Park, Wiltshire (103), as 'ruinous and in imitation of the Aqueducts of the Ancients'. Another is Sir John Soane's formal and serene Roman piece for Chillington Park, Staffordshire, of three semi-circular arches and a central temple (102). One of the earlier park bridges was the Grand Bridge of 1711 at Blenheim designed by Vanbrugh for the first Duke of Marlborough (41). It may be mentioned here again because it was never completed according to the architect's theatrical desires with a tall arcade and four towers 80 feet high. We can now see only the lower part of the ponderous structure and only the upper part of that, for its rooms, including a small theatre, have long since been half-submerged in an aquatic gloom by the lake created by Capability Brown.

A number of modern projects have been designed, most of them without hope of realization but merely for some purpose of commercial publicity. The Glass Age Development Committee, for example, has given us a lively scheme for a Thames road bridge in London, called the Crystal Span (107), bearing a seven-storey building enclosed in an air-conditioned glass envelope within which is included an hotel, art gallery, shopping arcade, open-air theatre and roof gardens – an enormous housed bridge like the Old London. And then there are several projects for a Channel bridge, one 25 miles long and composed of two decks slung between 24 suspension spans 250 feet above the sea – a forceful symbol of European unity. A Thames bridge which may, sooner or later, be achieved, is that across the proposed Thames Barrage at Woolwich.

We can continue to scheme and dream for the art of bridging will continue until the human span is crossed.

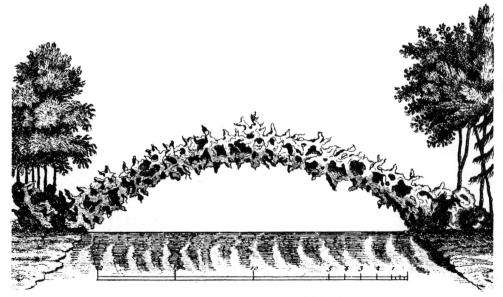

Elevation

102 Sir John Soane's dignified design for a bridge at Chillington House, Staffordshire.

Projects
101 *Below left*, a rococo footbridge from Over's *Ornamental Architecture*, 1758.

103 *Below*, a project by Robert Adam of 1786 for Bowood Park, Wiltshire, 'ruinous and in imitation of the Aqueducts of the Ancients'.

Plan and Elevation for a Bridge over the River Avon at the Rocks of St. *Bristol Hot W.*

Ground Plan and R.

Nº 20

Nº 1

INSCRIP: ANG: CONST.

ENGINE

13

MU. LIB.

12

MARINE

11

MANUF.

10

MANUF.

9

STONE WH.

8

W. Bridges, Invent. et Delin.

16

Demensions. The Great Arch 220 ft high 180 ft wide, Base 400 ft Long 140 ft wide, Roa

Contents Nº 1. A Light House. 2. A Toll House. 3. A Chapel, called St Vincent's. 4.5.6. Publick Grana

& a Stone Wharf & Water Mill. 9.10 Manufactories for Cotton, Wool, &c. 11. A Marine School. 12. A Mu

16. Twenty Houses in the Side of the Bridge. 17. Various Recesses for Out Offices, Stabling &c. 18. Clock Tu.

110

nt, from Sion Row Clifton, to Leigh Down, near
ENGINE
T COMS.
ST VINCENT
PUB.GRA
PUB:GRA
CORN.EX
COAL.WH
P.D. BRISTOL. Jany. 1793.
700 ft Long 50 ft wide, Each Story 40 ft high, Gallery 6 ft wide.
rn Exchange for foreign Grain; 7, Coal Wharf & General Market,
rary, & Subscription Room. 13, 14, Engine Rooms, 15, Vertical Windmills,
Case, 19, Watch House & Bellfry, 20, Road and Ground Plan.

104 William Bridges' masonry fantasy for the Avon Gorge, Bristol, of 1793, with central arch of 180 feet span – almost a small town.

London projects
105 Telford's design for a single iron span of
600ft to replace Old London Bridge; the high
approaches necessary prevented its adoption.
106 *Right*, George Dance's layout for a new
Port of London with its pair of bascule bridges
(depicted in an aquatint of 1800 by William
Daniell); on the left is the Monument and on
the right a new obelisk to commemorate the
naval victories.

107 A modern fantasy called the Crystal Span offered by the Glass Age Development Committee to cross the Thames where Vauxhall Bridge now stands. Its seven stories, enclosed in a glass envelope, would include an hotel, art gallery, shopping arcade, open-air theatre and roof gardens. It is a clumsy affair without gaiety but interesting as a development of the ancient housed bridges such as Old London Bridge. (Photograph: *The Times*)

108 *Page 116*, the new Severn Suspension Bridge seen in dramatic silhouette. (Photograph: British Steel Corporation)

Gazetteer

This selective list of existing bridges, old and new, in England, Scotland and Wales, should be marked 'E. & O.E.'. The author would welcome letters from readers who discover any serious errors or omissions in case of a reprint.

Counties are arranged alphabetically and bridges appear in historical order except in the two cases of the Thames, both in London and on the upper river, where they are listed in geographical order going upstream.

The figures at the ends of entries refer to numbers of plates.

England

BEDFORDSHIRE

Bedford Bridge. 1813.
Of Bedford stone in five segmental arches of classical design. Carries the A6 between Luton and Kettering across the Ouse. JOHN WING of Bedford.

CAMBRIDGE: The Backs

Clare Bridge. c.1640.
The oldest along the Backs. Three segmental arches of stone with decorated balustrades, which may be the first of their classical sort in the country. A delight. THOMAS GRUMBOLD (52).

St John's Bridge. c.1698.
Similar in style to Clare but more elaborately decorated. Three segmental arches with rusticated voussoirs, balustraded parapets and panels carved in bas-reliefs. Attributed to Wren but probably by his assistant NICHOLAS HAWKSMOOR.

Trinity Bridge. 1760.
Three segmental arches of stone with solid parapets ending satisfactorily with horizontal curls. JAMES ESSEX (53–4).

Queens College Bridge. 1749.
A Mathematical Bridge of timber trusses forming a single span. Based on truss designs of Palladio. JAMES ESSEX (51).

King's College Bridge. 1818.
Single low segmental span of stone with delicate mouldings. Simple and pleasing. WILLIAM WILKINSON.

New Bridge. 1826.
Single arch roofed and fenestrated in Gothic style. THOMAS RICKMAN and HENRY HUTCHINSON. (Rickman was an early Gothic revivalist who gave us the terms Early English, Decorated and Perpendicular, categorizing developments of Gothic style.)

Garrett Hostel Bridge. 1960.
Single 80ft span in prestressed concrete to replace cast-iron bridge of 1837. Elegant and pleasing case of early prestressed bridge with bronze railings and stone abutments. GUY AND TIMOTHY MORGAN (109).

109 Right, *Garrett Hostel Footbridge, Cambridge.* (Photograph: Edward Leigh, FIBP, FRPS)

CHESHIRE

Dee Bridge, Chester.
Late 13th century. Mostly red sandstone with seven pointed arches of varying spans and broad cutwaters. Defoe: 'A noble stone bridge over the River Dee, very high and strong built'.

Marple Aqueduct. 1802.
Solid masonry with pierced spandrels carrying Cotton-king Samuel Oldknow's Peak Forest Canal across river (60).

Grosvenor Bridge, Chester. 1834.
Single segmental arch, 200ft span, widest stone arch in the world until General Meigs completed Cabin John Bridge, Washington DC, in 1864 with a single span of 218ft. Handsome piece with classical trappings and a pair of Roman arches over footpaths at each end. Mainly Peckforton stone with some Scottish granite and some Chester red stone. Complete arch is in fact 230ft, for it continues beyond jambs of abutments. THOMAS HARRISON, born Richmond, Yorks, who also designed Chester Castle in Doric style as a prison and a number of other bridges; also country houses. (Grosvenor Bridge begun 1827 when he was nearly 80) (12).

Congleton Viaduct.
Typical long round-arched viaduct of the early railways striding powerfully across open countryside.

Stockport Viaduct.
Another typical viaduct of early railways, dramatic in scale in immutable landscape of grimy brickwork. Electrical excrescences now mar its skyline (110).

Manchester Elevated Road. 1960s.
Viaduct of 32 spans mostly of 105ft, composed of twin parallel prestressed concrete decks resting on tapering columns.

Runcorn–Widnes Bridge. 1961.
Replaced Widnes Transporter Bridge across Mersey. Two-pinned, bowstring, lattice-work steel arch with deck at high level. Main span 1082ft with side spans each 250ft. End cantilevers. One of MOTT, HAY AND ANDERSON's fine feats (89).

Hollow–Wood Farm Footbridge. 1963.
Main span 115ft of post-tensioned concrete box beam with steps at each end. Remarkable for its slimness. Crosses M6 motorway on its North Cheshire section.

Interchange Bridges, Birmingham– Preston Motorway, Cheshire section. 1963.
Carry interchange roundabouts. *In situ* post-tensioned box beams in two-span arrangements with row of central columns.

CORNWALL

Wadebridge.
15th century. Of local stone 400ft long with 15 (originally 17) pointed arches of 18ft 6in spans. Widened 1847 with segmental arches so reducing the projections of the cutwaters and spoiling the original design. With Bideford, Devon, it is one of the two longest bridges of the southwest. Carries the A39 between Camelford and St Columb.

110 Stockport Viaduct, Cheshire.

Gunnislake Bridge. c.1530.

Of white granite with six slightly pointed arches of varying spans, longest at 21ft. A beauty with bold cutwaters rising to refuges. Carries A390 between Liskeard and Tavistock on Devon border. (Similar bridges across Tamar are Greystone, between Tavistock and Launceston, and Horse Bridge, Stoke Climsland).

Royal Albert Railway Viaduct, Saltash. 1859.

Of two great iron fish-bellied girders with elliptical tubes as top members, approached by a series of iron beams resting on tall granite piers (79). A Victorian grotesque, next to Clifton Suspension, BRUNEL's most famous structure. Close to it also crossing the Tamar is the modern suspension road bridge, called Tamar.

Tamar Bridge, Saltash. 1961.

Central span of 1100ft. Towers of reinforced concrete, main cables being of wire ropes, and deck of reinforced concrete slab supported on steel stringers. Close to Brunel's Royal Albert.

CUMBERLAND

Lanercost Bridge. 1724.

Two bold segmental arches of 67ft spans and broad cutwater rising to a retreat. Takes road between Brampton and Lanercost Abbey across Irthing. Nearby are relics of an ancient bridge. possibly Roman (111).

DERBYSHIRE

Bakewell Bridge.

Mediaeval. Stone with five unusually regular pointed and ribbed arches with triangular cutwaters rising to refuges. Widened in 19th century. Carries road to Baslow across Wye (7).

Edensor Bridge, Chatsworth Park. 1683.

Graceful single, ribbed masonry arch of 66ft span flanked by two projections rising to refuges. Centre of parapet pointed. Carries A623 between Rowsley and Baslow across Derwent.

Sheepwash Bridge, Ashford.

Possibly 17th century. Three low segmental arches. Rough stonework with curious curving parapet wall at one end forming a sheepwash. Fits snugly into delightful landscape. On road to Sheldon (112).

Chatsworth Park Bridge. 1762.

Classical stone design of three arches and projections with niches at each end and statues above the two cutwaters. JAMES PAINE for Duke of Devonshire.

Kedelston Hall Bridge. c.1770.

Park bridge of three segmental arches with niched piers decorated at parapet level with swags and other refined details of period. ROBERT ADAM, who designed the Hall (45).

111 Lanercost Bridge, Cumberland.

112 Sheepwash Bridge, Ashford, Derbyshire.

St Mary's Bridge, Derby. 1788.
Three semi-circular arches of stone making civilized design. At town end 14th-century chapel of former mediaeval bridge.

Railway Viaducts, Chapel-en-le-Frith.
Mid-19th century. Pair of impressive converging viaducts with high arches of stone (81).

DEVONSHIRE

Post Bridge, Dartmoor.
Unknown date, could be 2000 years old. Most famous of clapper bridges. Spans River Dart near Princeton-Mortonhampstead road. Derives name from granite posts set up in district to guide wayfarers to bridge in snow or darkness. Four great granite slabs about 15ft wide resting on two piers and two abutments of rough granite rocks, the whole being held together by sheer weight (5). (Two smaller slab bridges of granite on Dartmoor are that over the Wallabrook and the rugged Teignhead Bridge, south of Fernworthy.)

Bideford Bridge. 1315.
Crosses Torridge with 24 Gothic arches of stone, not one arch being same size as another. The whole 677ft long. Widened 1815 and again in 1923 (with concrete corbels). Possessed a chapel at one time and as a toll bridge provided handsome profits which the feofees gave to education, charity and some good dinners.

Holne Bridge.
15th century. Rough granite bridge of four arches, widest being 34ft. A pleasing Ancient Monument. Takes A384 between Ashburton and Princeton across Dart.

DORSET

Sturminster Newton Bridge.
Mediaeval. Fine bridge over the Stour, of six pointed arches across river and to the north a stone causeway with ten semi-circular arches built 1828. Has been widened over the cutwaters.

Crawford Bridge.
Mediaeval, rebuilt in 16th century. Nine segmental stone arches across Stour and three brick flood arches. Four bold triangular cutwaters and refuges on upstream side.

113 Elvet Bridge, Durham.

COUNTY DURHAM

Elvet Bridge, Durham. 1225.
Ten pointed and ribbed arches of stone across River Wear. Was once housed like London Bridge and had a chapel at each end and a defence tower. Widened with round arches 1805 (113).

115 Tyne Bridge, Newcastle, Durham.

Barnard Castle Bridge.
Probably 15th century. Two masonry arches with skew arch at one end across Tees (114).

Prebends Bridge, Durham. 1772.
Three segmental arches. Recently restored.

High Level Bridge, Newcastle. 1849.
ROBERT STEPHENSON's double-decker taking railway on top and road below high above Tyne. Six bowstring arches of cast iron each spanning 125ft held in at bottom by wrought iron members with vertical rods of wrought iron. First application of bowstring arch. Nasmyth's Titanic Steam Hammer used for first time here in piling. (Between Tyne Bridge and High Level Bridge is a pivoting road bridge of iron of 1876).

Tyne Bridge, Newcastle. 1928.
Bowstring girder having widest steel arch span in Britain at 531ft. Heavy architectural towers. Useful type for heavy industrial traffic. MOTT, HAY AND ANDERSON (87–8, 115).

Kingsgate Footbridge, Durham. 1965.
Links two groups of college buildings across Wear. Strange, interesting design of reinforced concrete by OVE ARUP AND PARTNERS. Thin white band built on bank sides and then swivelled into place in two halves on two tall tapered fingers. 350ft long (94).

New Scotswood Bridge, Newcastle. 1968.
Steel tied arch of bowstring girder spanning 140ft.

116 Bourton-on-the-Water, Gloucestershire

Severn Suspension Bridge. 1966.
Magnificent ethereal structure with central span of 3240ft and side spans of 1000ft. Pull of catenary held by massive concrete anchorages. Towers 445ft high of steel portal frames. 18,000 miles of high-tensile steel wire used in cables, deck being shallow box of welded steel plates rigid enough to deal with aerodynamic problem. As an aid to this suspenders of steel wire rope from catenary to deck are not hung vertically but form narrow triangles. Carries M4 motorway (London to South Wales) over Severn between Aust and Beechley. MOTT, HAY AND ANDERSON with FREEMAN, FOX AND PARTNERS (85, 90, 108).

HAMPSHIRE

Northam Bridge, Southampton. 1960s.
Five spans, three of 105ft and two of 85ft. Important as first major prestressed concrete bridge in Britain. Takes coastal traffic between Southampton and Portsmouth.

HEREFORDSHIRE

Wye Bridge, Hereford. c.1490.
Of sandstone rubble faced with ashlar. Six round arches with cutwaters rising to refuges. Widened early 19th century. Main traffic now carried by new neighbour of 1966.

Wilton Bridge, Ross-on-Wye. 1597.
Red sandstone of six spans, five of round, ribbed arches. Strong character with large triangular cutwaters splayed at tops to form half-hexagonal refuges (117).

Bridstoe Bridge. 1960.
Prestressed concrete beams with anchor cantilever and suspended spans. Beautiful bridge with long, low main span of 203ft, whole integrating well with lovely landscape around. Carries Ross-on-Wye bypass over Wye about a mile from Ross.

GLOUCESTERSHIRE

Eastleach Martin Bridge.
Unknown date. Clapper bridge of five spans.

Bourton-on-the-Water, Cotswolds.
Late 18th century. Delightful collection of small footbridges of wrought stone (116).

Mythe Bridge, Tewkesbury. 1826.
Cast-iron bridge of single low segmental arch spanning Severn in a leap of 170ft. Six main ribs between stone abutments. TELFORD.

Cumberland Basin Swing Bridge, Bristol. 1960s.
Essential part of a major redevelopment for heavy local traffic, through traffic and shipping into City Docks. Long balanced cantilever of twin box girder construction on centre bearing, operated by hydro-electric power.

Almondsbury Interchange. 1960s.
Dramatic four-level steel and concrete structure connecting M4 with M5 motorway.

Winterbourne Railway Bridge. 1960s.
Crosses M4 motorway. Interesting as a fairly rare example of welded, portal frame uncovered steelwork. Main girders, each 254ft long, and piers make two parallel, three-span rigid frames with sloping legs.

117 Wilton Bridge, Herefordshire.
(Photograph: Reece Winstone)

HUNTINGDONSHIRE

Huntingdon Bridge. c.1370.
Of stone with decorative moulding in form of a trefoil corbel carrying upstream parapet over two of the six wide, pointed arches. Formerly possessed a chapel dedicated to St Thomas of Canterbury. Oliver Cromwell was born at Huntingdon and must have used the bridge often in his youth and may have returned there in 1645, the first year of the Civil War, when the third arch was temporarily replaced by a draw-bridge.

St Ives Bridge. 1426.
One of few mediaeval bridges still retaining a chapel. Six pointed arches, some ribbed, with debased chapel at centre, now a museum. Crosses the Ouse (26).

KENT

East Farleigh Bridge.
14th or 15th century. Finest mediaeval bridge in south. Kentish ragstone of four pointed arches and a small pointed arch over towpath. Four arches have narrow chamfered ribs. Massive cutwaters on both sides but no parapet refuges. Crosses Medway between East Farleigh and Barming, near Maidstone.

Eynsford Bridge.
Probably 17th century. Packhorse bridge in Kentish ragstone with brick and rubble parapets. Two semi-circular arches of 10ft spans.

Kingsferry Lifting Bridge. 1960.
Important modern lifting bridge carrying road and rail over River Swale between Kent and the Isle of Sheppey. Lifting span rising vertically between reinforced concrete towers has 90ft wide and 95ft high navigational clearance. No beauty but useful. MOTT, HAY AND ANDERSON.

Medway Bridge, Maidstone. 1963.
Two almost equal spans of 145ft and 125ft of post-tensioned beams and cantilevers with piers and foundations of reinforced concrete. Carries Maidstone bypass over Medway two miles downstream from Maidstone.

Medway Bridge and Viaducts. 1963.
Grand, elegant work carrying M2 across Medway near Rochester. Prestressed concrete canti-levered central span of 500ft is longest of its kind in world. Total length with approach viaducts 3340ft. FREEMAN, FOX AND PARTNERS.

Swanscombe Cutting Footbridge. 1960s.
Beautiful post-tensioned concrete span of a three-hinged arch with cantilevered spans. Crosses the A2. J. S. BERGG (21).

LANCASHIRE

Wycoller Village.
Seven small bridges and a ford with stepping stones. Clam bridge of single span and a clapper bridge of three spans. Village formerly a centre of communication on which moorland tracks converged; became busy place of hand-weaving before power-driven looms. Near Yorkshire border and associated with Brontës, Wycoller Hall being the Ferndean Manor of *Jane Eyre*.

Lune Aqueduct, Lancaster. 1796.
Solid classical work of stone having five semi-circular arches each of 75ft span. Carries Rennie's Lancaster Canal across River Lune.

Barton Swing Aqueduct. 1894.
Carries Bridgewater Canal across Manchester Ship Canal. Replaced Brindley's 'Castle in the Air' aqueduct of stone across River Irwell. Steel lattice with pivoting trough which can be swung open full of water, the whole weighing 1500 tons. Ends of trough closed with gates held by tapering wedges weighing twelve tons each and worked by hydraulic rams (62).

Samlesbury Bridge. 1958.
Three spans of 120, 180, 120ft of continuous welded steel box girder construction with con-crete piers and abutments faced with Yorkshire stone. Carries M6 over Ribble and the A59.

Lune Bridge. 1959.
Reinforced concrete open spandrel fixed arch of 230ft span, composed of two parallel arches of cellular construction. Light and simple. Carries M6 over Lune about two miles from Lancaster.

Thelwall Bridge. c.1960.
Riveted and welded steel with main span over Manchester Ship canal of 336ft. Deck slab of reinforced concrete. About three miles east of Warrington.

Gleaves Hill Bridge. c.1960.
Three-span continuous prestressed concrete of portal type having inclined legs and side span, deck soffit being curved. Centre span 143ft. Carries Preston–Lancaster motorway over M6 about six miles south of Lancaster.

Gathurst Viaduct. 1962.
Four spans of 150ft and two end spans of 100ft. Deck of welded girders 10ft deep supporting a reinforced concrete deck. Concrete piers. Carries M6 over River Douglas, Leeds–Liverpool Canal and a railway line.

LINCOLNSHIRE

High Bridge, Lincoln.
Mediaeval with later additions. There were shops on the bridge in 1391 but existing buildings on it were not built until 1540 when bridge was widened. A single arch of 23ft 6in at one end and 15ft 6in at other.

West Rasen Packhorse Bridge.

Date unknown. Of stone across River Rase with three ribbed arches. 4ft 6in wide.

Crowland Bridge.

Probably late 14th century. A stone curiosity also called Trinity Bridge or Three-Ways-to-Nowhere. Of rough limestone, it has three branches rising steeply to meet at middle and three arches between the branches forming Gothic points at the crowns. Originally spanning the confluence of three streams which are now dry, it stands as a purely decorative National Monument in the centre of a small fenland town. Each arch has three stone ribs with rough mouldings unusual in mediaeval bridges. Possibly the monks of Crowland Abbey built it as a symbol of the Holy Trinity and it may have formed the base of a large canopied cross rising above the marshes. A rough statue with flowing robes stands against one parapet which may have come from Crowland Abbey church (31).

LONDON'S THAMES

Tower Bridge. 1894.

Last Thames bridge before the sea. Bascule with two rising decks of steel and two bold towers of steel framework faced with granite and Portland stone in kind of Flemish Renaissance style. Bascules formerly raised for shipping by hydraulic power but now by electricity. Two footway beams span the 200ft high up between the towers. SIR HORACE JONES, City Architect, and SIR JOHN WOLFE BARRY (15).

London Bridge. 1973.

Last of a long series on same spot since Romans first erected a wooden bridge here. Replaced Rennie's granite structure of 1831, now rebuilt in Arizona. A practical job without visual thrills. Three spans, central one being 340ft wide. Four prestressed concrete box beams in precast segments strung together with cables like beads form flat 'arches', which are in fact cantilevers with a central suspended span. Piers faced with axed granite; parapets of polished granite. HAROLD KING, City Engineer (99).

Blackfriars Bridge. 1869.

Replaced Robert Mylne's splendid stone structure of 1769. Five low iron arches. Piers embellished with fat columns of red granite supporting pedestrian refuges. JOSEPH CUBITT.

Waterloo Bridge. 1942.

Reinforced concrete of five main spans, widest being 250ft. London's most elegant and beautifully simple bridge (at least in look) in spite of 'architectural' confusions imposed on engineers who nobly solved the problem with use of vast quantities of steel reinforcement. Appearance suggests segmental arch construction; in fact, spans are made up of four main beams, each continuous over two spans with cantilevers pro-jecting to support suspended beam at centre. Spandrels faced with Portland stone. RENDELL, PALMER AND TRITTON (98).

Westminster Bridge. 1862.

Replaced Labelye's fine masonry structure of 1750 when it gave way in 1846 under growing scour. Seven low arches of cast and wrought iron with granite-faced brick piers. Centre span of 120ft. THOMAS PAGE.

Lambeth Bridge. 1930s.

Replaced P. W. Barlow's old suspension of 1862. Four low steel arches between concrete piers and abutments faced with granite. SIR GEORGE HUM-PHREYS, Chief Engineer to LCC.

Vauxhall Bridge. 1906.

Replaced London's first iron bridge completed in 1816. Five steel arches with concrete piers and abutments faced with granite, central span being 150ft. Bronze statues above the piers. First London bridge to carry tramway lines. SIR ALEXANDER BINNIE and SIR MAURICE FITZMAURICE, both Chief Engineers to LCC.

Chelsea Suspension Bridge. 1934.

Concise steel bridge which replaced Page's ornamental old iron suspension of 1858. G. TOPHAM FORREST and E. P. WHEELER.

Albert Bridge, Chelsea. 1875.

Endearing eccentric in iron; half suspension, half cantilever, and early case of stayed type. R. M. ORDISH (55).

Battersea Bridge. 1890.

Replaced the 18th-century wooden bridge depicted in Whistler's famous 'Nocturne' in the Tate Gallery. Dull but useful. BAZALGETTE.

Wandsworth Bridge. 1938.

Three arches. Replaced structure of 1873.

Putney Bridge. 1886.

Of granite, replaced old wooden structure of 1729. Widened 1933. BAZALGETTE.

Hammersmith Suspension Bridge. 1887.

Replaced Tierney Clark's elegant suspension of 1827, London's first of this type. Bold ornamented towers and anchorages of painted iron. SIR JOSEPH BAZALGETTE, of the Metropolitan Board of Works (precursor of LCC).

Chiswick and Twickenham Bridges. 1933.

Two reinforced concrete bridges, Chiswick having three arches and Twickenham two extra land arches. ALFRED DRYLAND, County Engineer of Middlesex.

London, general
Serpentine Bridge, Hyde Park. 1826.

Delightful small masonry bridge of five segmental arches with classical balustrade. GEORGE RENNIE, son of John.

Wharncliffe Viaduct, Hanwell. 1837.

One of BRUNEL's fine arched viaducts for his Great Western Railway.

Holborn Viaduct. 1869.

Carries main road to the City over the valley, now underground, of the Fleet River, above which Farringdon Street runs. Part of a local replanning scheme opened by Queen Victoria on same day she opened Blackfriars Bridge at end of street. Splendid Victorian piece of decorated ironwork embellished on top with statuary.

St James's Park Footbridge. 1958.

Replaced Rendel and Wyatt's much mourned small iron suspension of 1857, but a functional, graceful little design of reinforced concrete with main span of 70ft. MINISTRY OF WORKS.

UPPER THAMES

Richmond Bridge. 1777.

Masonry faced with Portland stone, five segmental arches. One of several of its dignified kind across the river. PAINE AND COUSE.

Staines Bridge. 1831.

Fine granite bridge of three segmental arches, central one spanning 74ft and two side arches 66ft. Cutwaters of unusual design. GEORGE RENNIE, son of John.

118 Marlow Suspension Bridge, upper Thames.

Runnymede Bridge. 1961.

Low single arch of 173ft 6in with small arches in abutments. Eighteen encased steel arch ribs and reinforced concrete deck. Facing of Portland stone trim and red handmade bricks. Simple and elegant. Carries Staines bypass over Thames at Bell Weir. C. W. GLOVER AND PARTNERS.

Windsor Bridge. 1824.

Cast iron arches on granite piers. Iron now cracked and bridge limited to foot passengers and bikes, thus happily saving locality from ravages of the motor moloch.

Thames Bridge, Maidenhead. 1960s.

Elegant single arch spanning 270ft in welded steel with small side spans of 38ft, the whole faced with brick. Carries M4 motorway a mile south of Maidenhead. FREEMAN, FOX AND PARTNERS.

Maidenhead Railway Viaduct. 1830s.

One of BRUNEL's three viaducts of red engineering brick carrying the Great Western Railway over the Thames, the two others being at Basildon and Moulsford. Noble structure of two semi-elliptical arches each of 128ft span, one providing a fascinating towpath echo (13).

Maidenhead Bridge. 1772.

Classical masonry of seven wet and eight dry arches having Portland stone facing. SIR ROBERT TAYLOR, architect.

Marlow Suspension Bridge. 1832.

Stone towers with arches, and iron suspension of 218ft span. Makes delightful river picture with neighbouring church spire, long weir and general boskage. TIERNEY CLARK (118).

Henley Bridge. 1786.

Of Portland stone with five arches, very graceful with two keystone heads of Isis and Tamesis carved by Hon. Mrs Damer, cousin of Horace Walpole. HAYWARD.

Sonning Bridge.

18th century. Lovely rich red weathered brickwork of eleven irregular arches rising to centre.

Shillingford Bridge. 1827.

Good classical masonry design with three main arches and ten small flood arches.

Abingdon Bridge. 1416 and later.

Two sections, one over navigable river, other over millstream. Originally had pointed arches but widened upstream with round arches in 1790 and later was given a main wide arch. Main bridge reconstructed 1926 but ancient irregular character largely retained by reinforced concrete faced with local stone preserved from old structure. Main bridge now has one wide arch and four small ones, while millstream section has seven pointed arches.

Donnington Bridge, Oxford. 1962.

Ten portal frames comprising horizontal prestressed concrete beams supported at each end of pair of triangulated inclined legs. Single span of 170ft crossing river on skew and forming part of inner relief road.

Folly Bridge, Oxford. 1827.
Four spans of stone. On site of mediaeval bridge which had a watchtower let in 17th century to one Welcome, thus providing name Welcome's Folly.

Thames Bridge, Oxford. 1961.
Twelve two-pinned prestressed concrete portal frames cast *in situ* of 140ft span. Carries Oxford Southern and Western bypass.

Swinford (Eynsham) Bridge. 1777.
Pleasing classical design of ashlar masonry with nine round arches by the EARL OF ABINGDON. Toll house at one end. Carries the A40.

New Bridge, Kingston Bagpuize. c.1250.
Six pointed arches of rough stone with cutwaters carried up as refuges. Originally ribbed but ribs removed in 1793 to aid navigation. Largely reconstructed in 15th century and again in 1801. Said to be oldest bridge over Thames, but Radcot, higher upstream, may be older; hence name New.

Radcot Bridge.
Probably early 13th century, and so oldest bridge across Thames. Local stone with three arches, two being pointed. From a wharf by the bridge, Upton stone for building St Paul's Cathedral was loaded on to rafts to be floated down to London. Carries A4095 between Bampton and Faringdon (32).

Lechlade Bridge. 1792.
Attractive stone bridge with single segmental arch and two small towpath arches. Sometimes called Halfpenny Bridge on account of toll formerly charged.

NOTTINGHAMSHIRE

West Bridge, Clumber. 1798.
Classical style built for Duke of Newcastle on his estate. Three raised segmental arches 13ft 6in wide of brick and stone. Widened 1931. Carries A614 between Nottingham and Doncaster across River Poulter.

Winthorpe Bridge. 1960s.
Three-span continuous prestressed concrete with centre span of 260ft. Low and elegant. Carries Newark bypass over Trent.

Clifton Bridge, Nottingham. 1960s.
Prestressed concrete with main span of 275ft consisting of two cantilevers and a 100ft suspended span. Fine example of its decade.

NORTHAMPTONSHIRE

Irthlingborough Bridge.
Probably 14th century. Mostly stone of nineteen arches. Triangular refuges remain on downstream side. Restored 1925. Carries A6 between Irthlingborough and Higham Ferrers.

Wansford Old Bridge.
13th, 16th, and 18th centuries. Eleven arches of varying spans, largest being 50ft. Carries A6118 between Huntingdon and Stamford.

NORTHUMBERLAND

Twizel Bridge.
Date unknown but mediaeval character. Graceful single stone arch of 90ft span across Twill between Berwick-on-Tweed and Cornhill. Economical ribbed vaulting (24).

Warkworth Bridge.
14th century. Two wide segmental arches of 60ft span each across River Coquet; of local sandstone. Defensive gateway at one end. Fine broad cutwater with recess at top.

Old Bridge, Berwick-on-Tweed. 1624.
Dressed sandstone of fifteen low segmental arches.

Corbridge. 1674.
Seven segmental arches of stone with heavy piers, carrying A69 between Newcastle and Hexham across Tyne.

Lion Bridge, Alnwick. 1773.
Of dressed local sandstone beside Alnwick Castle with three arched spans, centre 50ft wide crossing River Aln between Newcastle and Berwick. Guarded on parapet by the Northumberland lion with poker tail outstretched.

Cupola Bridge. 1779.
Fine simple job of three segmental arches of dressed sandstone carrying A686 between Hexham and Alstone across West Allen River.

OXFORDSHIRE

Grand Bridge, Blenheim Park. 1711.
Vanbrugh's theatrical baroque gesture in stone crossing a lake in the Duke of Marlborough's park. Never completed owing to the Duchess's contempt for its extravagance (40–1).

Magdalen Bridge, Oxford. 1779.
Fine classical stone bridge with six round arches, carved keystones, balustrade, and rusticated columns at piers. Widened 1882, but original design preserved. Crosses the Cherwell, tributary of the Thames. JOHN GWYNN (3, 33).

119 Detail, Coalport Bridge, Shropshire.

tions held together with iron keys and screws. Built across Severn by ironmaster ABRAHAM DARBY (58–9).

Welsh Bridge, Shrewsbury. 1795.
Five segmental stone arches. Simple, with pleasing proportions. TILLY AND CARLINE.

Dinham Bridge, Ludlow.
18th century. Simple stone of three segmental arches across Teme.

Coalport Bridge, Coalbrookdale. 1818.
Somewhat like Iron Bridge, showing little development in technique. About one mile downstream from Iron Bridge (119).

Stokesay Bridge. 1823.
Cast iron ribs on masonry abutments with single span of 54ft 9in. Carries A49 across River Onny between Shrewsbury and Ludlow. TELFORD.

Severn Bridge, Shrewsbury. 1964.
Low elegant arches of reinforced concrete. Deck prestressed longitudinally. Carries Ditherington-Monkmoor road over Severn.

SHROPSHIRE

Ludford Bridge, Ludlow.
Bulky piers suggest Norman period. Stone of three semi-circular ribbed arches each 30ft span across Teme. Once graced with a chapel (25).

English Bridge, Shrewsbury. 1774.
Seven stone arches crowned with balustrade and decorated with carved dolphins on the cutwaters. Central arch 50ft wide. Reconstructed 1927 to increase width and reduce hump-back. JOHN GWYNN, who also designed Magdalen Bridge, Oxford, Atcham near Shrewsbury, and Worcester (4).

Atcham Bridge, near Shrewsbury. 1776.
Seven spans in Grinshill stone rising in size towards centre. GWYNN's most beautiful design with good detailing. Carries London–Holyhead road across Severn. (New concrete bridge nearby of clumsy design built in 1920s) (50).

Tern Bridge, Atcham. 1778.
Elegant structure in Grinshill stone with balustrades, carved keystones and niches at abutments of single segmental arch of 90ft span. Carries London–Holyhead road. WILLIAM HAYWARD.

Iron Bridge, Coalbrookdale. 1779.
First bridge in the world made wholly of iron. Five semi-circular ribs forming single arch of 100ft 6in span. Spandrels filled with iron circles and ogee Gothic arches and deck of cast-iron plates covered with slag and clay. Each of arch ribs cast in two parts. Precast parts floated down river and whole completed in three months. Designer thinking in terms of masonry and carpentry. Joints dovetailed and rectangular sec-

SOMERSET

Tarr Steps, Winsford, Exmoor.
Unknown date, possibly 3000 years old. Low clapper bridge with 17 spans, total length being 180ft. Clapper stones weigh four or five tons each. Crosses the River Barle on the track to Hawkridge. Referred to in *Lorna Doone* as a Devil's bridge. Very picturesque in deep wooded valley.

Horner Water, West Luccombe, Allerford, and Dunster, Exmoor.
Each village has its packhorse bridge: the one at Dunster, called Gallox Bridge, has two arches with slightly pointed tops and double arch rings.

Petherton Bridge.
Possibly 15th century. Rough stone structure crossing River Parrett and carrying the Fosse Way. Pair of quaint, worn stone figures built into the end of a parapet. Thomas Gerard (1633): 'A faire stone bridge, at the end of which I have seen graven on a stone the effigies of the founder and his wife, now much defaced by lewd people, and the memory of them for want of an inscription lost'.

Clifton Suspension Bridge. 1836-1864.
BRUNEL's most famous structure swung high over the Avon Gorge of iron suspension between two stone towers. Original design, considerably altered in the event, won in competition to which Telford also contributed a design. Bridge not completed until after Brunel's death. The chains from the old Hungerford Bridge, London, also by Brunel, were used when that was demolished to make way for the existing railway bridge. Span of 702ft, the Somerset end being three feet lower than the Gloucester end, a

deliberate subtlety instigated by Brunel to counter the effect produced by the land configuration (69).

Bath

Prior Park Palladian Bridge. 1756.
Built for Ralph Allen as an almost exact copy of the Palladian Bridge, Wilton Park, designed by LORD PEMBROKE, the Architect Earl, helped by Robert Morris. Sophisticated classical structure with a colonnade and roof.

Pulteney Bridge. 1769.
The only housed bridge, excepting High Bridge, Lincoln, left in Britain, in a tradition going back to the lakeland village. Designed by ROBERT ADAM in his refined classical style, it was built under patronage of Sir William Pulteney after the Avon had been made navigable up to Bath and when Pulteney had decided to link his Bathwick estate with the city. Of Bath stone on three arches bearing two-storeyed shops and houses. The weir below the bridge was admirably re-designed in 1972 as part of a flood protection scheme by Neville Conder and F. Greenhalgh, a scheme which received a Civic Trust Award (47).

Cleveland Bridge. 1833.
Originally an arched cast iron bridge designed by HAZZLEDINE. Reconstructed 1930 with help of reinforced concrete so that bridge retains its pristine look. Carries A3080 across Wiltshire Avon.

North Parade Bridge. 1836.
Handsome cast iron arch rib bridge with single span of 111ft. Probably also by HAZZLEDINE. Crosses Avon within the city.

STAFFORDSHIRE

Shugborough, or Essex, Bridge.
16th century or earlier. Stone of 14 arches and triangular cutwaters with refuges, whole being low and 312ft long with width between parapets of only 4ft. A bridle or packhorse bridge crossing Trent in Shugborough Park near Great Haywood.

Viator's Bridge, Milldale.
Unknown date. Pack-horse bridge across River Dove at northern end of Dove Dale. Rough stone of two segmental arches. Izaak Walton: 'Why, a mouse can hardly go over it'.

SUSSEX

Stopham Bridge.
Possibly 16th century. Picturesque in Sussex sandstone with seven main arches with semi-circular heads and one larger, taller central arch which is segmental and turned in brick, perhaps of later date than other arches built high to aid navigation. Nine recesses for pedestrians. Crosses River Arun on A283 between Pulborough and Petworth (35).

Balcombe Viaduct.
Mid-19th century. Magnificent example of railway engineering with its long rhythm of brick arches. A remarkable perspective below bridge with its row of voids arched above and below. Takes the old London, Brighton and South Coast Railway across the Ouse Valley (80).

WARWICKSHIRE

Old Stare Bridge.
Late 13th century. Built by Cistercian monks of Stonleigh Abbey. Sandstone ashlar with nine pointed arches of about 12ft span. Enormous cutwaters with refuges above as wide as the arches.

Clopton Bridge, Stratford-upon-Avon. 1480.
At one time even longer than Bideford Bridge, Devon, at 1100ft. Now only 500ft. Shakespeare must have crossed it many times. Of ashlar masonry of fourteen spans each about 19ft wide, all arches being pointed. Widened 1811. Financed by Sir Hugh of Clopton, Mayor of London, who bought New Place, Stratford from Shakespeare (120).

Warwick Castle Bridge. 1793.
Grey sandstone with single arch unusually wide for period at 105ft. Carries A41 between Warwick and Banbury across Avon.

Tramway Bridge, Stratford-upon-Avon. 1823.
Simple bridge of red brick with seven semi-elliptical arches originally built to carry a horse tramway.

WESTMORLAND

Crook-of-Lune Bridge.
Probably 17th century. Two segmental arches of rough masonry crossing Lune between Grayrigg and Sedbergh.

Bridge House, Ambleside, Lake District.
Date unknown. A curiosity with rubble-stone cottage supported on an arch across a stream said to have been built thus by owner to avoid taxes. Now office of National Trust.

WILTSHIRE

Bradford-on-Avon Bridge.
14th century. Nine arches of stone and a charming small oratory (only one of its kind), having a dome added in the seventeenth century when bridge was widened. Oratory became a lock-up in 18th century and John Wesley was interned there for a night in 1757.

Lacock Bridge.
Date unknown, probably mediaeval. Four pointed arches of stone. Attractive small bridge. Carries road between Lacock and Bowden Hill.

120 Clopton Bridge, Stratford-upon-Avon, Warwickshire.

Combe Bissett Bridge.
Mediaeval packhorse bridge of stone across Avon. Three pointed arches and no parapets (to avoid scraping of projecting packs); now has wooden railings. 6ft wide. One side refaced with brick. (Close by is a modest eighteenth-century road bridge of three arches).

Wilton Park Palladian Bridge. 1737.
Elaborate, classical, roofed bridge of decorative kind with Ionic portico, balustrades, carved keystones and rusticated pediment. Outstanding product of Age of Taste and landed aristocracy. Built by ninth EARL OF PEMBROKE, the Architect Earl, one of the first landscape gardeners who superintended the construction of Labelye's Westminster Bridge, London. Probably designed the bridge himself with the aid of Robert Morris, Copies stand at Stowe and Prior Park, Bath (44).

WORCESTERSHIRE

Pershore Old Bridge.
Mediaeval. Stone with brick parapets. Six round arches, centre spanning 27ft 6in.

Worcester Bridge. 1781.
Stone of five arches each 40ft span. Widened and reconstructed 1932 in concrete faced with stone. JOHN GWYNN.

Bewdley Bridge. 1799.
Sandstone of seven spans across Severn, longest being 59ft 6in. Strengthened 1926. TELFORD.

Holt Fleet Bridge, Ombersley. 1828.
Single low arch spanning 150ft of cast iron with open spandrels and sandstone abutments. Crosses Severn. Strengthened 1928. TELFORD.

Knightsford Bridge. 1959.
Three-span, cantilever type with centre span of 90ft. Superstructure of reinforced concrete cellular construction. Piers, abutments and training walls of mass concrete faced with brickwork. Civic Trust Award 1959. Carries Worcester–Bromyard road (A44) over Teme at Knightwick, nine miles west of Worcester.

Queenhill Bridge. 1960s.
Mostly concrete with three central spans of steel. 2466ft long in 27 spans on a curve. Carries Ross Spur motorway (M50) over Severn, about three miles north of Tewkesbury.

YORKSHIRE

Wakefield Chantry Bridge.
Mid-14th century. Stately stone bridge of twelve pointed arches. West elevation of chapel restored by Scott, 1847 (27).

Rotherham Chantry Bridge. 1483.
Formerly across River Don but now no water flows below its four pointed arches (28).

Knaresborough High Bridge.
Mediaeval of two arches, older one being ribbed. Crosses Nidd on Harrogate–Knaresborough road. Widened 1826.

Barden Bridge.
Mid-17th century. Pleasing masonry of three segmental arches across River Wharfe on Barden-Appletreewick road.

Ferry Bridge, Knottingley. 1797.
Dignified design of rusticated masonry with three segmental wet arches and a number of dry ones. Takes A1 across Aire between Doncaster and

121 Middlesbrough Transporter Bridge, Yorkshire.

Wetherby. JOHN CARR, architect, of York, who designed Harewood House and mansion at Basildon Park.

Nidderdale, West Riding.
Two packhorse bridges, one at Thronthwaite, other at Haxby across Nidd between Burnt Yates and Birstwith. Latter a beautiful, humpbacked, single span of 63ft.

Middlesbrough Transporter Bridge. 1911.
Spans 470ft between steel towers 225ft above Tees high water. Cantilevers of steel taking travelling car (121).

Wharfe Bridge, West Riding. 1959.
Reinforced concrete of cantilever and suspended span with central span of 160ft. Suspended span of 70ft of precast post-tensioned I-beams. Elegant. Carries A1 over Wharfe on Wetherby bypass.

Wentbridge Viaduct. 1961.
Reinforced concrete, 470ft between outside bearings with pair of inclined, tapering legs between prestressed deck of cellular construction. Centre span of 190ft. Grand, simple design. 90 miles of steel tubing used for scaffolding during construction. Carries A1 over Went Valley (97).

Tinsley Viaduct, Sheffield. 1967.
Composite of steel and concrete. Spans Don Valley with two decks carrying M1 motorway on upper level and all-purpose road below.

Scotland

ABERDEENSHIRE

Balgownie Bridge, near Aberdeen. c.1320.
Built, according to legend, by order of Robert the Bruce (122).

Dee Bridge. 1527.
Seven ribbed arches. Widened 1841.

Brig o' Dye, near Aberdeen.
Possibly late 17th century, but mediaeval character. Single arch of 43ft span.

ARGYLL, INVERARAY

Aray Bridge.
18th century. Stone with pierced central spandrel. Attributed to ROBERT ADAM (46).

AYRSHIRE

Brig of Ayr.
13th century. Restored 1910 in memory of Robert Burns and his poem 'The Brigs of Ayr'.

Brig o'Doon, near Ayr.
15th century. Five single round-arch span of 70ft. Monument nearby to Robert Burns whose ballad 'Tam O'Shanter' describes an incident on the bridge when Tam is pursued by warlocks in the mirk.

Howford Bridge, Ayr. 1962.
Reinforced concrete of single span of 300ft with open spandrels. In spectacular Ballochmyle gorge on Kilmarnock–Dumfries road.

BERWICKSHIRE

Berwick Old Bridge. 1624.
Fifteen spans.

Coldstream Bridge. 1766.
Crosses Tweed on Northumberland border. Five arches with tunnelled spandrels. JAMES SMEATON (38).

Kelso Bridge. 1803.
Five arches of 72ft span each. One of first in Britain to carry level roadway and to contain elliptical arches. Forerunner of London's Waterloo. JOHN RENNIE.

Union Bridge. 1820.
449ft span across Tweed. First suspension to take carriages. SIR SAMUEL BROWN (123).

Royal Border Bridge. 1850.
28 semi-circular stone arches of 60ft span rising 126ft above Tweed Valley. ROBERT STEPHENSON.

EDINBURGH

Dean Bridge. c.1800.
One of TELFORD's best masonry bridges with four tall arches rising 100ft above the Water of Leith (124).

Forth Railway Bridge, near Edinburgh. 1890.
Cantilever and beam of steel. BAKER AND FOWLER (9, 83–4).

Forth Road Bridge, near Edinburgh. 1964.
Steel suspension with span of 3300ft. FREEMAN, FOX AND PARTNERS with MOTT, HAY AND ANDERSON (93).

122 Below, *Balgownie Bridge, near Aberdeen.*
123 Right, *Union Bridge, Berwickshire.*
(Photograph: Adam J. Scott)

124 Dean Bridge, Edinburgh.

FIFESHIRE

Guard Bridge. 1450.
Well built of six irregular arches in stone.

Tay Road Bridge. 1960.
Connects Fifeshire with Dundee. Steel and concrete 7365ft long with 42 spans. W. A. FAIRHURST.

GLASGOW

Clyde Street Footbridge.
Early 19th century. Iron suspension between classic stone towers decorated with Ionic columns.

Erskine Bridge. 1972.
Nine miles west of Glasgow across Clyde. Fine steel and concrete structure with approach viaducts. Centre span supported by two stayed girders of steel.

INVERNESS-SHIRE

Craigellachie Bridge. c.1800.
Trussed iron arch of 152ft span with castellated stone abutments. First truly modern bridge of iron. TELFORD.

Ness Bridge, Inverness. 1961.
Three-span prestressed concrete with centre span of 120ft.

KIRKCUDBRIGHT

Tongueland Bridge. 1805.
Single masonry span of 112ft across Dee with hollow spandrels. TELFORD.

LANARKSHIRE

Mouse Water Bridge, Cartland Craigs.
Immensely tall stone arches across wooded gorge. TELFORD.

PERTHSHIRE

Millhaugh Old Bridge, Glenalmond. 1619.
Single, graceful arch of 63ft span, with cutwaters and refuges each end. Pierced spandrels.

Aberfeldy Bridge. 1733.
One of General Wade's military bridges in scheme for opening up Highlands. One of very few with baroque character (37).

STIRLING

Stirling Bridge. c.1400.
A war bridge of strategic importance as it is the lowest crossing of the Forth. Until the late eighteenth century almost only access to north of Scotland (30).

Wales

BRECKNOCKSHIRE

Taf Fechan Bridge. 1960s.
Between Hirwaun and Abergavenny. One of three reinforced concrete, open-spandrel fixed arch bridges in the Heads of the Valleys. Curved on plan with span of 227ft. Built by cantilever construction with cables instead of staging (95).

Taf Fawr Bridge. 1960s.
Crosses tributary of River Taff 110ft above valley. Also balanced cantilever construction. Three box girder spans, centre of 216ft. Elegant.

Nant Hir Bridge. 1960s.
On Heads of the Valleys road. Similar to Taf Fechan, with concrete arch of 184ft.

CAERNARVONSHIRE

Waterloo Bridge, Bettws-y-Coed. 1815.
An iron curiosity by TELFORD taking Holyhead road across Conway River. 105ft arch span with brilliant casting which reads 'This Bridge was constructed in the same year the Battle of Waterloo was fought'. In each spandrel the rose, thistle, shamrock, and leek are brightly painted. Strengthened recently by having interior ribs unobtrusively encased in concrete (74).

Conway Suspension Bridge. 1826.
TELFORD's iron suspension between castellated towers below Conway Castle. Next to it Conway Tubular and modern steel arch road bridge of 1958 (70).

Menai Bridge. 1826.
TELFORD's suspension masterpiece crossing Menai Straits and linking Anglesey to mainland on Holyhead road. Central span between masonry towers 579ft. Refurbished 1940 by Sir Alexander Gibb whose great-grandfather had been Telford's resident engineer on building of Aberdeen Harbour (67–8, 125).

Conway Tubular Bridge. 1848.
GEORGE STEPHENSON's railway structure similar to Britannia in principle but lower and smaller, single span of two tubes, each 412ft long (77).

Britannia Railway Bridge. 1850.
GEORGE STEPHENSON's famous structure of iron tubes of four spans between stone towers, two main ones 460 ft, across Menai Straits near Menai Bridge. Damaged by fire caused by children in 1970, pristine form now marred by supporting arch (8, 76, 78).

CARMARTHENSHIRE

Dolau-Hirion Bridge. 1773.
Single segmental arch of 84ft span, with pierced haunches across the Towy near Llandovery. WILLIAM EDWARDS of Pont-y-Pridd fame.

Llandeilo Bridge. 1848.
Widest and highest single span of its masonry type in Wales.

DENBIGHSHIRE

Llangollen Bridge.
Part 1131 but largely rebuilt mid-14th century and again about 1500. Irregular of four arches.

Holt Bridge. 1545.
Low red sandstone of eight arches and pleasing proportions. Originally strategic with drawbridge, tower and gateway.

Bangor Isycoed Bridge.
17th century. Fine design of red sandstone crossing Dee with five segmental arches and shallow refuges. Attributed to INIGO JONES.

Llanrwst Bridge. 1636.
Also called Pont Fawr, or the Great Bridge. Masonry with centre span of 60ft and side spans of 45ft with segmental arches. Elegant design in spite of undressed ashlar. Known as Shaking Bridge since it vibrates if parapet above centre arch is struck. Also attributed to INIGO JONES.

Chirk Aqueduct. 1801.
Ten round-headed stone arches of 40ft span each carrying iron trough to reduce weight which puddled clay would impose. Carries Welsh Section of Shropshire Union Canal over Ceiriog. TELFORD.

125 Menai Straits Bridge, Caernarvonshire.

126 Thomas Telford.

Chepstow Bridge. 1816.
Open ironwork of five spans across Wye (73, 127).

Pant-y-Goytre Bridge. c.1821.
Fine stone bridge across Usk with tunnels in spandrels. JOHN UPTON of Gloucester (39).

Newport Transporter Bridge. 1906.
Elegant steelwork with beam 177ft above water carrying hanging carriage across 145ft span. R. H. HAYNES and Frenchman F. ARNODIN (designer of Pont Transbordeur, Marseilles, destroyed in Second World War) (17).

George Street Bridge, Newport. 1960s.
Cable cantilever design with main span of 500ft across Usk. Ropes of steel wire, deck of cellular steel boxes, towers of hollow concrete (92).

Wye Viaduct. 1960s.
Ten steel spans and a stayed girder across Beachley Peninsula west of Severn bridge carrying M4 motorway (91).

Coldra to Crick.
On London–South Wales motorway. 1960s. Eleven underbridges, six overbridges and two viaducts, all of interest.

Pont Cysylltau Aqueduct. 1805.
Four miles from Chirk taking the Welsh Section of the Shropshire Union Canal across River Dee. Exposed iron trough on iron arches carried on 18 slender masonry piers at 127ft above river. 1000ft long. Walter Scott: 'The most impressive work of art I have ever seen'. Next to Menai Bridge, TELFORD's masterwork (61).

FLINTSHIRE

Queensferry Bridge. 1960s.
On Queensferry bypass, built to be converted later into a vertical lifting bridge. Three spans of welded plate girders.

GLAMORGANSHIRE

Pont-y-Pridd. 1750.
Most beautiful single-span bridge in Britain and landmark in bridge construction on account of its high arch of 140ft span across River Taff. Haunches pierced with tunnels. WILLIAM EDWARDS, farmer and mason (1).

Neath Bridge. 1955.
Carries bypass over River Neath between Briton Ferry and Earlswood. Reinforced concrete, three-quarters of a mile long.

MONMOUTHSHIRE

Monnow Bridge, Monmouth.
1272 but widened later. Best preserved war bridge in Britain with tower. Ribbed arches (29).

Usk Bridge. 1563.
Sturdy with seven segmental arches. Widened 1794.

127 Chepstow Bridge,
Monmouthshire.

128 Next page,
Spettisbury Bridge,
Dorset. (Photograph:
B. C. Clayton)

DORSET
ANY PERSON WILFULLY INJURING
ANY PART OF THIS COUNTY BRIDGE
WILL BE GUILTY OF FELONY AND
UPON CONVICTION LIABLE TO BE
TRANSPORTED FOR LIFE
BY THE COURT
7&8 GEO 4 C30 S13   T FOOKS